P9-CCV-138

Geo-Texas

Number Eighteen:
W. L. Moody, Jr.,
Natural History Series

Eric R. Swanson

Geo-Texas
A Guide to the Earth Sciences

Texas A&M
University Press
COLLEGE STATION

Copyright © 1995 by Eric R. Swanson
Manufactured in the United States of America
All rights reserved
Third Printing, 2001

The paper used in this book
meets the minimum requirements of the
American National Standard
for Permanence of Paper
for Printed Library Materials,
Z39.48-1984.
Binding materials have been chosen for durability.
♾

Library of Congress Cataloging-in-Publication Data

Swanson, Eric R., 1946–
    Geo-Texas : a guide to the earth sciences / Eric R.
Swanson. — 1st ed.
        p.   cm. — (W. L. Moody, Jr., natural history
series ; no. 18)
    Includes index.
    ISBN 0-89096-663-X (cloth). — ISBN 0-89096-
682-6 (pbk.)
    1. Earth sciences—Texas.   I. Title.   II. Series.
QE167.S93   1995
557.64—dc20   95-12488
                                                                CIP

For Jenny and Travis

Contents

Tables

Preface

Texas has 350 miles of coastline, sports ninety-one mountain peaks a mile or more above sea level, and spans ten climatic zones. Texas is among the nation's leading states in the production of petroleum, sulfur, helium, granite, and many other natural resources. The state has the biggest fossil pterosaur, the greatest number of caves, the most tornadoes, the nation's greatest 24-hour rainfall on record, the most meteorites, rocks of every geologic age—and some major environmental problems as well. Texas has world-class oceanographic institutions, Johnson Space Center, and McDonald Observatory, casting its giant eye toward worlds light-years away. But where can the average citizen learn more about these and other topics having to do with Texas earth science?

Earth scientists in Texas work at universities, for state and federal agencies, in public and private research institutions, for companies of all sizes, and as independent consultants. They generate an enormous amount of information, and they love to talk and write about it. But they talk mostly to other scientists, and most of what they write ends up in the hands of other specialists or in dark corners of university libraries—which is where most of it belongs. Some of what these folks know, however, is extremely interesting and important to the general public. An ocean of information exists, yet only a trickle of watered-down data has managed to leak into the popular scientific literature.

This book originally was conceived as a way to give Texas teachers and students access to that information and allow teachers to teach and students to study examples of earth science phenomena occurring in Texas. As the project unfolded, however, it became clear that the information would have wide appeal. The result is an earth science book written uniquely from the Texas perspective, for teachers, students, and anyone else interested in Texas natural history.

The ten chapters in this book are arranged like those in typical earth science textbooks. First comes a discussion of astronomy and related topics. The connections between Texas and the cosmos are many, and some have included disasters of immense proportions. Next, an outline of the physiographic provinces of Texas lays the groundwork for subsequent chapters covering a wide variety of Texas weather topics and 1.5 billion years of Texas geologic history.

Chapters 5 through 8 delve more deeply into aspects of Texas geology, starting with volcanoes and earthquakes. Many people do not realize that Texas can have earthquakes and volcanoes. In 1931, West Texas was rocked by the Valentine quake, which had an estimated Richter magnitude of 6.0, and El Paso residents live within a stone's throw of extremely young volcanic activity. To delight rock hounds, chapter 6 deals with minerals, rocks, and fossils. The chapter also addresses that favorite topic, dinosaurs. The state's natural resources are covered in chapter 7, with particular attention to the fascinating history surrounding the discovery of petroleum in Texas. Ground water resources—a subject of increasing importance—and caves are discussed in chapter 8. Chapter 9 dives into oceanography, a significant field of earth science study, and into the Gulf of Mexico, an important Texas resource. The closing chapter deals with the timely topic of the state's environmental problems.

The six appendixes are filled mostly with information on how to get more information. Included are addresses of Texas rock-hound clubs and geological societies, as well as information about earth science careers and a list of Texas colleges and universities offering earth science programs. There is a catalog of free or inexpensive sources of educational material pertaining to earth science. The book even has an appendix that can be used as an earth science travel guide to Texas.

Much of the information in this book has been culled from the work of others, and authors to whom I am indebted are cited in the text and in a bibliography at the end of each chapter. This book was a joy to write; it is meant to make enjoyable reading as well.

Acknowledgments

This book would not have been possible without the contributions of many individuals and institutions. Its content reflects decades of work by dedicated geoscientists too numerous to mention. A special group, however, consists of the geologists and staff of the Texas Bureau of Economic Geology—many of whom are now "working the other side of the range," to use the vernacular of frontier mining men. Wayne Gordon, past president of the Science Teachers Association of Texas, suggested the need for a source of information to help teachers answer their students' Texas earth science questions. Larry Butts of the Texas Natural Resource Conservation Commission, Sandra Barnes and Thomas G. Barnes III of McDonald Observatory, and Philip D. Rabinowitz of the Ocean Drilling Program, headquartered at Texas A&M university, all provided information on the activities of their respective organizations. Ann Cook of the Texas Department of Transportation was of enormous help in providing access to photographs, and Nancy Place of San Antonio's University of Texas Health Science Center adroitly made the switch from physiology to physiography to prepare the line drawings. At this point, most authors acknowledge—eagerly, it seems to me—all errors to be solely their responsibility. I reluctantly accept that blame and request that readers employ only humane means in bringing errors to my attention.

Geo-Texas

1 Texas and the Universe

Houston, Tranquility Base here.
The Eagle has landed.
—Astronaut Neil Armstrong, July 20, 1969

Most books about the science of the Earth begin with astronomy and related topics, including the Moon, asteroids, comets, meteorites, space exploration, and the origin of the universe. They may also explain how the tilt of Earth's axis produces our seasons and how gravitational tugs from the Moon and the Sun produce our daily coastal tides.

But how can such topics be viewed from a Texas perspective? True, Texas has approximately twelve thousand square miles of tidal wetlands and seasons that seem to change in a day. But what more is there in Texas that we can properly relate to the rest of the universe?

Our state is large, more than seven hundred miles from Texarkana to El Paso and over eight hundred miles from the North Texas line at Texline to our southernmost town of Southmost. Still, these are hardly cosmic proportions. Light, for example, speeding at 186,000 miles per second, can cycle between Texline and Southmost nearly 120 times a second. What in Texas, then, besides its citizens' legendary bravado, is of cosmic proportions? How much astronomy can there be, after all, in a place called the Lone Star State?

A clue to the surprising answer may be found in the first words uttered on the moon—words directed at Houston, Texas. Much of what is known about the universe has been discovered at Texas-based institutions such as Johnson Space Center and McDonald Observatory (fig. 1.2). Their impact on science has been enormous.

Speaking of impact, Texas is one of only two states where you can stroll through an actual meteorite crater. There are at least two other places in Texas where meteors hit Earth as well (fig. 1.1). Viewing the results of cosmic collisions is exciting, but rock exposed along the banks of the Brazos River goes beyond exciting—all the way to chilling. Sedimentary rocks there tell of an enormous ancient impact, and they foretell how

3

FIG. 1.1. Texas cosmic institutions and meteorite impact sites.
Map by Nancy Place.

human life on Earth may end. This chapter, then, explores the interesting, exciting, frightening, and very real connections between Texas and the universe, starting with some "cosmic" Texas institutions.

McDonald Observatory

Everyone knows the old song: "The stars at night are big and bright, deep in the heart of Texas." Nowhere in the state, however, do the stars shine more brightly than atop Mount Locke, where McDonald

FIG. 1.2. McDonald Observatory, atop Mt. Locke in the Davis Mountains of West Texas. Courtesy *Texas Highways.*

Observatory is located (fig. 1.1). At 6,809 feet above sea level, the observatory lies ten miles northwest of Fort Davis. This McDonald's has no golden arches, but its W. L. Moody, Jr., Visitors Center serves over 100,000 visitors annually. *Big and Bright* is the title David Evans and Derral Mulholland chose for their 1986 book tracing the interesting history of McDonald Observatory.

William Johnson McDonald was a prosperous banker from Paris, Texas, who died in 1926. He left the bulk of his fortune, over one million dollars, to the regents of the University of Texas for the "purpose of aiding in erecting and equipping an astronomical observatory," to quote from his will. Distant relatives contested the will, partly on the grounds that the old gentleman was of unsound mind when he made the bequest. The university contended that a donation to astronomy did not necessarily imply insanity and ultimately settled for approximately $800,000. This was a large sum in those days, but one vexing problem remained. The University of Texas, at the beginning of the Great Depression, was not exactly the center of the scholarly astrophysical universe. Ultimately, the University of Texas and the University of Chicago banded together to create what became one of the world's largest university-operated observatories. The first dome was dedicated in 1939. It housed an advanced model of Isaac Newton's invention, the reflecting telescope. The telescope's 82-inch (2.1-meter) mirror was, at the time, the world's second largest. The program quickly accelerated, and, while most large observatories ceased operations during World War II, the 82-inch reflector played a major role in laying the foundations of modern astrophysics.

The University of Texas assumed sole control over operations at Mc-Donald Observatory in 1962; and in 1969 a larger dome, with a 107-inch (2.7-meter) reflector, was dedicated (fig. 1.3).

Did I say 107 inches? Actually, today the reflector measures only 106 inches. In 1970, a newly hired employee (from Ohio) went berserk and unloaded his pistol directly at the 107-inch mirror. The damage turned out to be minimal. The resulting craters were bored out and painted black, diminishing the light-gathering power of the mirror to the equivalent of a 106-inch instrument.

Thousands of discoveries large and small have been made at McDonald Observatory. Among them are oxygen in the atmosphere of Mars, small amounts of water vapor on Mars and Venus, and methane ice on Pluto's surface. McDonald also pioneered laser ranging experiments that measure, to within inches, the distance between Earth and reflectors left by astronauts on the Moon. Laser ranging has revolutionized our knowledge of the Moon's orbit and our understanding of wobbles in the rotation of both Earth and Moon, and it has documented the existence of earth tides. Earth tides are similar to ocean tides, but the tidal bulge moves across the land surface, rhythmically opening and closing the distance between Earth and Moon by a foot or so. The laser program helped to confirm Einstein's Theory of General Relativity. It also forms part of a worldwide system involved in laser ranging to artificial satellites. Other laser ranging applications include measuring continental drift and determining various geophysical properties of Earth by their effects on orbiting satellites.

The 107-inch reflector was the world's third largest telescope when it was built, and it still ranks among the twenty largest. In addition, there are one 36-inch and two 30-inch reflectors at the complex. Another instrument at McDonald is the millimeter-wave dish (fig. 1.4). It looks like a 16-foot satellite dish, but its gold-plated surface reflects millimeter

FIG. 1.3. The 107-inch reflecting telescope at McDonald Observatory gath-
ers a quarter of a million times more light than the human eye.
Courtesy McDonald Observatory, University of Texas at Austin.

Fɪɢ. 1.4. The millimeter-wave dish at McDonald Observatory collects radio waves from space.
Courtesy *Texas Highways.*

waves emitted by interstellar dust. Interstellar dust is both the product of super novae and the stuff of which new stars are made. All these instruments and McDonald's remote location make it one of the best astronomical observatories in the world.

At Marfa, forty miles south of McDonald, the University of Texas operates what is called "the Two-Mile Telescope." It is not the ultimate reflector but an array of antennae in eight straight lines. The signals they detect have a wave length of roughly three feet and come from quasars and galaxies with active nuclei. Quasars are objects of extreme power and distance. Although some emit a thousand-trillion times more energy than the sun, the energy received on Earth was generated over ten billion years ago, long before Earth existed. The minute amount of energy received from such a incredibly distant object is hard to imagine; astronomers estimate that, if the Two-Mile Telescope had been operating since the beginning of time, it would not yet have gathered enough energy to burn a light bulb for a single second! Analyzing the energy generated by these distant objects is like looking into the distant past. While true time travel remains the stuff of science fiction, astronomers at McDonald and Marfa now use their instruments to look at the universe as it existed billions of years before humans walked the Earth.

In the Caucasus Mountains of the former USSR, at 6,830 feet above sea level (21 feet higher than McDonald), sits the last of a generation of giants. Its 236.2-inch (6-meter) mirror, more than twice the diameter of McDonald's largest instrument, is said to be capable of locating objects down to the 25th magnitude. That's like detecting the light from a candle at a distance of 15,000 miles! Since it weighs seventy-eight tons, however, gravity distorts the mirror's shape as it moves, blurring its images.

The Russian colossus is probably the last of its type, as technological breakthroughs are now ushering in a new age of superoptical telescopes. In 1993, the Keck telescope (the Keck Foundation is a private philanthropic organization), with its revolutionary thirty-six hexagonal mirrors, joined a cluster of other astronomical instruments high atop Hawaii's Mauna Kea. Mauna Kea, rising 13,600 feet above sea level, stands above 99 percent of Earth's atmospheric water vapor; hence the "seeing" conditions there are excellent. The Keck telescope's three dozen segments form a 10-meter mirrored surface, twice that of the venerable Hale Telescope on Mount Palomar, California, and 4 meters more than the one-eyed Russian giant. The segmented design makes for much lighter mirrors, and computers are used to control changes in mirror shape. At the time of this writing, the Keck is unique, but at least a dozen other super telescopes are being constructed or are planned. Their locations are divided about equally between Hawaii's Mauna Kea, Chile's high Atacama Desert, and the continental United States. Arizona might receive several super telescopes, and Texas is building one of its own.

The University of Texas at Austin and an international coalition of universities are in the process of placing a super telescope near the McDonald facilities on Mount Locke. Dubbed the Hobby-Eberly telescope, its segmented primary mirror will be composed of ninety-one 1-meter mirror sections, the equivalent of an 11-meter (432-inch) instrument. The Texas-size telescope will exceed all existing telescopes in its ability to image and perform spectroscopic analysis of light gathered from faint and distant astronomical objects. Spectroscopic analysis investigates the nature of an object by examining the quantity and nature of the light emitted by it. This information is used to answer questions about the origin, evolution, relative velocity, and composition of such objects. Applications include investigations of stellar evolution, measurement of astronomical distances and velocities, inquiries concerning the mysterious dark matter that seems to permeate the universe, and the search for planets.

McDonald Observatory is keenly aware of its public responsibility, a responsibility arising from William McDonald's founding bequest. In 1973, the observatory began publishing a monthly newsletter which has become *Star Date*, a popular astronomy magazine available by subscription. "Star Date" is also the name of a radio series produced by McDonald and broadcast in English and Spanish by stations nationwide. McDonald Observatory maintains a public information service (telephone 512-471-5285) at its Austin headquarters and a visitors center on Mount Locke.

The visitors center serves as the observatory's check-in point and education center. It is also a celestialphile's shopping paradise, selling astronomical paraphernalia at down-to-Earth prices. The center hosts Star Parties on Tuesday, Friday, and Saturday evenings. Weather permitting, 14- and 24-inch telescopes are set up, and experts give guided tours of the night sky. Daytime programs feature a guided tour of the observatory and a view of solar activity using a 14-inch telescope (with protective filters in place, of course).

Once a month, McDonald does something that no other observatory allows. With advance reservations, the public can use the 107-inch telescope. Weather permitting, you can enjoy a spectacular view of Jupiter, Saturn, or a binary star. If the sky is cloudy, the staff's stellar performance still will dazzle you. Current information on programs and schedules may be obtained from the following address: W. L. Moody, Jr., Visitors' Information Center, Box 1337, Fort Davis TX 79734; tel. (915) 426-3263.

Johnson Space Center: A Race for Space

The Space Age probably began with the surprise launching in 1957 of a grapefruit-sized Russian satellite called Sputnik 1 (Schichtle 1983). One month later, the 1,120-pound Sputnik 2, containing a live dog, was launched; and in May, 1958, the Russians placed in orbit the 2,925-pound Sputnik 3.

Our nation was in shock. In addition to being left behind as the space race began, we worried about the Soviet Union's hydrogen bomb. Would they perhaps put a thermonuclear device in our backyard? Our first attempt to recover a position of superiority in space was embarrassing. In full view of the largest group of reporters yet assembled for such an event, a Vanguard rocket managed to rise only four feet before it fell back

Fɪɢ. 1.5. The Johnson Space Center near Houston, Texas.
Courtesy NASA.

in flames. The Russians were sympathetic, offering aid through a United Nations program to provide technical assistance to backward nations!

In reaction, Congress in 1958 formed the National Aeronautics and Space Administration (NASA), and in 1961 an incoming President Kennedy made it a national goal to put a man on the Moon before the end of the 1960s. In May, 1961, Alan B. Shepard, Jr., America's first man in space, took a fifteen-minute sub-orbital flight. Also in 1961, NASA announced that the manned spacecraft center would be located near Houston on land donated by Rice University (fig 1.1).

As a senator, Lyndon B. Johnson led an investigation into why the Russians had beaten the United States in the race to launch the first satellite. As vice president, he immediately was given responsibility for overseeing U.S. space efforts. The two-person Project Gemini, with its space "walks" and docking maneuvers, took place during the Kennedy-Johnson years. Apollo 11's lunar landing on July 20, 1969, took place just six months after President Johnson had left office. It was appropriate, then, that the Houston facility ultimately became the Lyndon B. Johnson Space Center (figs. 1.5 and 1.6).

Fɪɢ. 1.6. The Saturn V rocket at the Johnson Space Center's Rock Park measures 363 feet in length. Rockets of this type were used to launch America's manned lunar missions. Photo by author.

Lunar Samples

Between 1969 and 1972, six Apollo missions brought back two hundred separate samples weighing a total of 842 pounds (382 kg) from the lunar surface (fig. 1.7). Almost forgotten by this time were the 300 grams returned by three automated Soviet spacecraft. What has happened to the lunar rocks? Forty-eight large pieces were placed into nitrogen-filled glass display cases or embedded in clear plastic and put on public display worldwide. One large chunk is on permanent display at the Johnson Presidential Library in Austin. Most of the rest are at NASA's Lunar Sample Building at LBJ Space Center (fig. 1.8). The Sample Building's staff is responsible for preserving and protecting the specimens and making them available for scientific and educational purposes. Lunar samples are kept in cabinets filled with purified nitrogen gas, to prevent contamination by dust or reaction with atmospheric water and oxygen. Even after twenty years, most of the samples have not been analyzed. It is not that NASA scientists are not up to the task. Rather, Moon

FIG. 1.7. An Apollo 17 astronaut collects lunar samples in the Taurus-Littrow Valley of the Moon, December 13, 1972, for shipment to the Johnson Space Center near Houston. Courtesy NASA.

rocks tend to be in short supply, and samples need to be available for future studies as new theories and technologies emerge. Scientists from universities and research institutions around the world continue to study the lunar rocks. Every March, many of them convene at Johnson Space Center for the Lunar and Planetary Science Conference, and each year's contributions comprise a thick volume published shortly after the meeting.

Education is an important function of the Lunar Sample Building, and parts of it are open to the public. The staff also have prepared plastic discs containing lunar samples strictly for educational purposes (see appendix E for address). The discs contain the three most abundant lunar rocks—anorthosite, breccia, and basalt—as well as grains sieved from three types of lunar "soil." The samples are small and best viewed with a binocular microscope to see the rock textures and small surface craters

Fɪɢ. 1.8. A lunar rock
inside a nitrogen-filled
work station at the Johnson
Space Center's Lunar
Sample Building.
Photo by author.

(zap pits) caused by the impact of micro-meteorites. A slide show and taped narration accompanies each disc.

Johnson Space Center also houses an enormous collection of meteorites belonging to the Smithsonian Institution of Washington, D.C. The meteorites have been recovered in recent years from the surface of the Antarctic ice cap, and a few of them have rather surprising compositions. Scientists now are fairly certain that some of the meteorites are actually Moon rocks. They theorize that past lunar meteorite impacts managed to blast rock free from the Moon's gravitational field. Occasionally, these lunar meteors are intercepted by Earth, recovered by American scientists, and shipped to Houston where they live out their "lives" a stone's throw away from Astroworld. Also present is an extremely rare type of meteorite that some scientists think originated in meteorite impacts on Mars!

Texas Meteorites and Tektites

Although tiny meteors are constantly entering Earth's atmosphere and meteorite falls occur with some regularity, it is rare for a person to be hit. Towns in France and Mexico have been showered with meteorite

FIG. 1.9. Although found near Burlington in Milam County, this meteorite was named Rosebud when the name Burlington was found to be in use for a New York meteorite. The cone-shaped stony meteorite weighs just over 121 pounds and is eighteen inches wide (Bullard 1939). Its smooth, furrowed surface shows the effects of heat generated by passage through the atmosphere. It was presented to the University of Texas at Austin in 1915 and is believed to have fallen in 1908.

Courtesy Joe Jaworski, Department of Geological Sciences, University of Texas at Austin.

fragments with no casualties. The only American known to have been struck is Mrs. E. H. Hodges of Sylacauga, Alabama. In 1954, she survived a blow from an 8.5-pound meteorite that plunged through her roof. No one in Texas has yet been hit, but there have been a few close calls.

Texas, in fact, has more identified meteorite localities than any other state. Many of our state's meteorites are on display at local natural history museums (see appendix F for museum locations). One example was found in 1903 by a 7-year-old boy in Cherry Creek, eighty miles north of McDonald Observatory. This fine 1,530-pound specimen is on display at the McDonald visitors' center, and several meteorite specimens are exhibited in Austin at the Bureau of Economic Geology and at the University of Texas (fig. 1.9). Barnes (1939a) gives information on seventy different Texas meteorite localities, some with multiple specimens. Meteorites tend to have interesting stories surrounding their discovery. Here are a few such stories.

For years, the solid 25-pound stone had been used as a weight on the family's sauerkraut barrel. In 1936, however, it was identified as a meteorite, identical in appearance to several other stony meteorites found around the turn of the century near Cedar, southwest of La Grange, in

Fayette County. A prehistoric fireball meteorite apparently had shattered over the Texas Gulf Coastal Plain, scattering its fragments about.

A 320-pound stony meteorite (the Bluff meteorite), different in appearance, was found in 1878 just southwest of La Grange. Two additional fragments were identified in 1936, the same year as the "sauerkraut meteorite." One of the chunks, a 17-pound stone, had been plowed up and tossed into the weeds about forty years earlier. The old farmer, however, never forgot the strange rock he'd unearthed, and it was ultimately recovered. A troop of Boy Scouts discovered, also in 1936, a 102.5-pound stony meteorite about three miles south of Cuero in DeWitt County.

In 1915, an iron meteorite was found that is thought to have weighed about two tons. I say "thought" because the meteorite was not recovered and all attempts to relocate it have failed. It is believed still to lie where it landed, covered by debris in Juniper Canyon on the flanks of the Chisos Mountains in Big Bend National Park.

Occasionally meteorites are seen falling. Texas examples include a small stone that fell out of the sky near Kirbyville in Jasper County on November 12, 1906, and a 2.2-pound stone that dropped near Troup in Smith County on April 26, 1917. On the evening of January 21, 1922, an 8-pound stony meteorite fell on Florence in Williamson County, and on September 4, 1930, a 4.6-pound stony meteorite hit Plantersville in Grimes Country. None of these events, however, matched the splash made by the meteorite that fell on the Gage Ranch, nine and a half miles southeast of Marathon.

It was a hot August afternoon in 1946, and folks at the ranch had gathered around the headquarters swimming pool. Suddenly there was a sonic boom, a brilliant flash of light, and a sizzling sound. Astounded bathers watched as a meteorite scored a direct hit on the pool. No one was injured, but some twenty-four people were within a few hundred feet of the cosmic dunking. Numerous fragments, including one 104-pound chunk, were recovered, and the impact produced a small crater, slightly increasing the depth of the pool.

Large meteors tend to explode as fireballs, and several Texas fireball meteorites have been seen. Early in the evening of May 2, 1939, a bright meteor streaked southward across the Houston sky. It was visible for about three seconds and left a smoky trail that ended with a terrific explosion over Kendleton, a short distance southwest of Houston. After several minutes, fragments, some weighing several pounds, fell over a four-square-mile area surrounding the town.

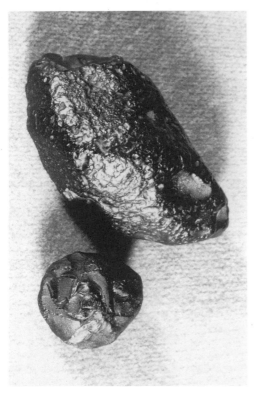

FIG. 1.10. These tektites from Fayette County, Texas, are considered to be the fused products of meteorite or comet impacts on Earth. Courtesy *Texas Highways.*

A fireball meteorite seen late in the afternoon on June 23, 1928, may have been even larger, but no fragments were recovered. Witnesses report that for several seconds the already bright South Texas sky was brilliantly illuminated as if by a second sun streaking through the atmosphere. The spectacle was visible from Corpus Christi, on the coast, to Brownwood, three hundred miles to the north. It left a long-lasting cloud in the atmosphere, and it made a whizzing or whining sound followed by a rumbling noise like explosions or distant thunder. The various sightings indicate that the meteor passed through the atmosphere between Uvalde and the small town of Cline, a short distance to the east.

Among the strangest types of meteorites are curiously shaped, glassy objects known as tektites (from the Greek word *tektos,* meaning melted) (Barnes 1939b). Tektites commonly are about the size of a walnut, are generally dark, and when unbroken they tend to be shaped like teardrops, spheres, disks, or even dumbbells (fig. 1.10). They are found in definite areas called strewn-fields, and tektites from each strewn-field are commonly given a distinct local name. North American tektites are extremely rare. One lone specimen was found at Martha's Vineyard, Massachusetts, and tektites from Georgia have been known since 1938. The first North American tektites, however, were discovered in Texas.

In the spring of that vintage year for meteorites, 1936, several strange glassy objects from east of College Station were shown to Bureau of Economic Geology personnel, who identified them as tektites. They have since been dubbed *bediasites*, for Bedias, a small town in Grimes County. Rock hounds report finding tektites near the small town of Dime Box (between Austin and College Station), as well as just east of College Station, around Bedias. The origin of tektites is a subject of controversy. There is general agreement that they are the chilled glassy products of rock melted and expelled as a result of the impact of very large meteorites. Most workers believe a responsible meteorite must have struck somewhere in the vicinity of the related strewn-field, but the source of the Texas tektites has yet to be identified. There are, however, three known Texas impact sites (fig. 1.1).

The Odessa Meteorite Crater

Four meteorite craters form a tight cluster about ten miles southwest of Odessa (Sellards and Evans 1941). The largest crater is still visible as a depression more than five hundred feet across and sixteen feet deep (fig. 1.11). The limestone forming the crater rim has been uplifted and locally tilted to nearly vertical position. The Odessa meteorite crater was discovered in 1921, and thousands of iron meteorite fragments, the largest weighing 206 pounds, have been recovered with the aid of powerful magnets and metal detectors. Studies at the site have shown that the main crater originally was about one hundred feet deep, and that three smaller craters lie buried nearby. The exact age of the meteorite fall is unknown, but it probably took at least several thousand years to fill all but the last sixteen feet of the largest crater. An age of about twenty thousand years is suggested by fossil bones found in the crater fill, including those of a primitive horse and an elephant!

Bee Bluff Impact Site

Bee Bluff is the name given to a probable impact site thirteen miles southwest of Uvalde on Highway 83 (fig. 1.1) (Wilson and Wilson 1979 and 1984). Although all traces of a crater have been removed by

FIG. 1.11. The Odessa Meteorite Crater, as seen from the air on
December 11, 1962. Courtesy *Texas Highways.*

erosion and the area is spectacularly unspectacular, the evidence is contained in the rocks. The impact site consists of a circular area of deformed and brecciated sedimentary rock, about 1.5 miles in diameter.
Sandstone layers at the site clearly have been disrupted, and quartz
grains in the rock display microscopic planar fractures believed to have
been caused by the shock wave associated with the meteorite's impact.
The age of the Bee Bluff impact is uncertain, but certainly millions of
years have passed since the devastating meteorite struck.

The Sierra Madera Structure

The Sierra Madera, located twenty miles south of Fort Stockton
at the northeastern end of the Glass Mountains (fig. 1.1), is no ordinary
hill. It is, rather, the deeply eroded remains of an impact site much larger
and older than the Odessa crater (Wilshire et al. 1972). The Sierra
Madera is at the center of a circular area of intensively deformed rock
more than seven miles in diameter. The hill itself rises six hundred feet
above the surrounding plain. It is the eroded three-mile-wide remnant

of a central peak of the type seen in large lunar craters. A surrounding low region of shattered rock and upturned rim complete the structure. The deep level of erosion indicates that the meteorite impact occurred many millions of years ago, but its exact age is not known.

Asteroid Impacts, Mass Extinctions, and the Brazos River K-T Boundary Layer

Asteroids are believed to be remnants of *planetesimals* (sun-orbiting bodies that are smaller than planets) left from a period of planetary formation about 4.5 billion years ago. Between the orbits of Mars and Jupiter lies a belt of asteroids ranging in size from more than six hundred miles in diameter down to the limits of detectability. Over ten thousand are known, and hundreds are discovered annually. There are other asteroids and the cores of degassed comets with more eccentric orbits. The paths of these bodies cross the paths of the inner solar system planets, including Earth, and they are known as the near-Earth asteroids (NEAs). More than 150 NEAs with diameters of half a mile (1 kilometer) or more have been charted. About a dozen or so are added to this list every year; the total number of NEAs is estimated to be about 1,300.

In 1980, a group of scientists shocked the scientific world by discovering a thin, iridium-rich layer of clay lying between fossiliferous rocks of Cretaceous age (given the symbol of K) and deposits from the Tertiary period (given the symbol T). Iridium is a rare element in most terrestrial rocks but not in meteoritic material. The iridium-rich "K-T boundary layer," as it came to be called, has been found worldwide (including in Texas), suggesting that the deposit was produced by an asteroid-sized impact.

Major geologic eras seem to end with mass extinctions. Could they be extraterrestrially inspired? Specifically, could some doomsday asteroid have been responsible for the mass extinction at the end of the Cretaceous period, the last period in which many creatures, including dinosaurs, lived? Geologists are now engaged in lively debate and research on that topic.

Sedimentary rocks around the margin of the Gulf of Mexico have been deposited continuously since Cretaceous time. These include rocks exposed along the Brazos River (fig. 1.1), where an unusual sandstone bed is found interlayered with an unusual mudstone. The sandstone has been interpreted as the product of a great *tsunami*, a wave estimated to have been 165 to 330 feet high! Mudstone overlying the giant-wave deposit is rich in iridium; that is, it is a K-T boundary layer. Evidence like that at the Brazos River site has suggested that an asteroid may have struck the Gulf of Mexico region, but proof has been difficult to find.

In 1991, an international team of scientists announced the discovery of a buried 110-mile-wide circular structure centered on the Yucatan Peninsula town of Chicxulub Puerto (pronounced cheek-shu-lub and meaning "tail of the devil" in Mayan). Although debate and investigations continue, the Chicxulub structure is believed by some to be the long-sought impact site responsible for the K-T boundary deposits and the trigger for the great extinction of species at the end of Cretaceous time.

Earth's upper atmosphere annually may experience as many as eighty blasts equal to that produced by a small atomic device. They are the products of rather large meteorites that heat up and explode with little or no harm to life below Earth's protective atmospheric shield. The most destructive historic example of this process seems to be the Tunguska fireball, a tremendous explosion over central Siberia in 1908. Apparently an aerial blast, it left no crater but felled trees and animals as far as forty miles from its center. It has been estimated that the explosion had the energy equivalent of more than twelve million tons of TNT, a hundred times the energy of either of the two atom bombs dropped on Japan in 1945. An impressive explosion, but no asteroid impact.

Asteroid falls must be extremely rare; there is no historic record of one hitting Earth's surface. Still, asteroids are out there, and our thin atmospheric shield offers little protection against their rare but inevitable arrival. Asteroid Eros, roughly twenty-two miles long, passed within fourteen million miles of Earth in 1975; and in January, 1991, the Spacewatch team at Kitt Peak watched as a thirty-foot rock passed between the Moon and Earth, a near miss by cosmic standards. In 1972, people witnessed and even filmed a large fireball blazing through the atmosphere over the northern United States and Canada before reentering space. The remarkable display apparently was the result of a glancing blow that allowed the meteor to skip off Earth's atmosphere like a stone on the surface of a pond. Of the asteroids that we have detected, these are some of the ones coming closest to Earth.

It is frightening to think about the near misses that occurred before such things were routinely monitored; and it is little comfort to remember that, in this cosmic game of bumper cars, the asteroid gets the worst of it. Texas has three known impact sites and the Brazos River K-T boundary layer—sober reminders of the truth in one geologist's statement, "Civilization exists by geological consent . . . subject to change without notice."

References

Barnes, Virgil E. 1939a. *Catalogue of Texas meteorites*. Publication No. 3945. Austin: Bureau of Economic Geology, University of Texas at Austin. 583–612.

———. 1939b. *North American tektites*. Publication No. 3945. Austin: Bureau of Economic Geology, University of Texas at Austin. 477–582.

Bourgeois, J.; Thor Hansen; Patricia Wiberg; and Erle Kauffman. 1988. A Tsunami deposit at the Cretaceous-Tertiary boundary in Texas. *Science* 241: 567–69.

Bullard, Fred. 1939. The Rosebud meteorite, Milam County, Texas. *American Mineralogist* 24 (no. 4): 242–54.

Evans, David, and Derral Mulholland. 1986. *Big and bright: A history of the McDonald Observatory*. Austin: University of Texas Press. 186p.

Schichtle, Col. Cass. 1983. *The National Space Program: From the fifties into the eighties*. National Security Affairs Monograph Series. Fort Lesley J. McNair, Washington, D.C.: National Defense University Press. 83–86.

Sellards, E. H. 1929. The Texas meteor of June 23, 1928. University of Texas Bulletin No. 2901. Austin: Bureau of Economic Geology, University of Texas at Austin. 85–94.

Sellards, E. H., and G. Evans. 1941. Statement of progress of investigation of the Odessa meteor craters. Austin: Bureau of Economic Geology, University of Texas at Austin. 1p.

Wilshire, H. G.; T. W. Offield; K. A. Howard; and D. Cummings. 1972. Geology of the Sierra Madera cryptoexplosion structure, Pecos County, Texas. United States Geological Survey Professional Paper 599-H. Washington, D.C.: U.S. Government Printing Office. 42p.

Wilson, W. F., and D. H. Wilson. 1979. Remnants of a probable Tertiary impact crater in South Texas. *Geology* 7: 144–47.

———. 1984. Meteor impact site, Anacacho asphalt deposits. *South Texas Geological Society Guidebook*. San Antonio: South Texas Geological Society. 97p.

2 Physiographic Provinces of Texas

> "What you Northerners never appreciate, Pearl, is that Texas is so big
> that you can live your life within its limits and never give a damn
> about what anybody in Boston or San Francisco thinks."
> —James A. Michener, *Texas*

Texas is a very large state with tremendously diverse climates and landforms. The state contains parts of the following five major North American
physiographic provinces: the Gulf Coastal Plain, the Interior Lowlands,
the Great Plains, the Rocky Mountains, and the Basin and Range
Province. And Texas can be carved into fifteen or more distinctive local
provinces. A fairly standard middle ground (Maxwell et al. 1970), and
the system adopted here, divides the state into eight physiographic
provinces (fig. 2.1). This chapter covers the landforms of Texas and tells
how those landforms came to be. We shall travel through them in a generally westward direction, starting with the Texas Gulf Coast. Ultimately
we shall reach the higher and drier westernmost regions, the lands that
gave rise to film stereotypes about the Lone Star State.

Gulf Coastal Plain

Texas' Gulf Coastal Plain (fig. 2.1) borders the western Gulf of
Mexico, in an arc 180 miles wide, from the Sabine River on the northeast to the Rio Grande border with Mexico (Morton 1988). The province
shows little topographic relief, but its surface rises gently inland to an
average elevation of about 500 feet above sea level in its northeastern
and central parts and increases to about 1,000 feet near Del Rio.

The coastal plain is the surface expression of a thick wedge of sediment dumped onto the subsiding Gulf of Mexico crust since Cretaceous time, more than sixty million years ago. The plain has been
created during Cenozoic time (the most recent geological era) by rivers eroding mountains to the west and transporting enormous volumes of sediment to coalescing deltas of the Gulf of Mexico. Below
the Gulf Coastal Plain, individual sedimentary beds dip, like the coastal
plain surface itself, gently toward the Gulf. From west to east, they

23

FIG. 2.1. Physiographic provinces of Texas.
Map by Nancy Place; adapted from Maxwell et al. (1970).

represent a succession of increasingly young sedimentary formations laid down in an imbricate fashion as the Gulf coastline migrated oceanward. That is to say, they lie like so many overlapping slices of cheese laid across a tray, the last one even now being deposited along the Texas Gulf Coast. These "cheese slices" are composed mostly of common sandstone, mudstone, and clay; they are spiced locally with

FIG. 2.2. Port Isabel and South Padre Island, a typical coastal barrier island and lagoon. Courtesy *Texas Highways*.

iron-stone, beds of low-grade coal called lignite, and deposits of uranium.

Today, enormous amounts of sand and silt continue to be supplied by the Sabine, Trinity, Brazos, Colorado, and Rio Grande rivers to nourish the deltas, barrier islands, and fringing lagoons that so characterize the Texas Gulf Coast (fig. 2.2). The Rio Grande, more than any other river, has produced a marked outward encroachment or delta into the Gulf of Mexico, forming what is known as the coastal bend. Other Texas rivers tend to lack deltas. Instead, barrier islands guard the estuarian entrances to these river systems. The estuaries and barrier bars are consequences of the relatively recent rise in sea level that began about eighteen thousand years ago, at the end of the last Ice Age. As the polar ice caps melted and retreated, global sea level rose and Gulf waters inundated coastal river valleys, forming bays and estuaries. Because rainfall was more plentiful at the end of the Ice Age, swollen rivers carried an abundance of sediment which nourished small deltas filling the bays. As the climate to the west became increasingly arid and less sediment reached the coast,

FIG. 2.3. Coastal erosion due to ground subsidence has caused the abandonment of this section of old Texas Highway 87 south of Beaumont.
Photo by author.

ocean currents reshaped the deltaic deposits into the barrier islands we see today. Padre Island is a prime example. Over the past five thousand years, it has grown to a length of 113 miles, making it the country's longest continuous barrier island (Weise and White 1980).

As rivers have been dammed in recent years, the natural reduction in sediment supply has been accelerated, and the construction of jetties has disrupted the longshore currents and restricted movement of sediment along the coast. The decline in sediment supply, combined with local surface subsidence problems, has contributed to some dramatic recent coastal erosion. The upper Texas coast along Texas Highway 87 is believed to be receding at an average rate of more than ten feet per year. The beach there has become narrow and steep. Now it also is littered with oil field production equipment, foundations and septic tanks from old beach houses, even abandoned remnants of Highway 87 (fig. 2.3). It may appear that sea level is on the rise, but that is just an illusion. The sea is coming in, but the sea's encroachment is due mainly to land subsidence caused by the compaction of underlying sediment and to beach erosion resulting from the reduction in sediment supplied by rivers.

An average of about 50 inches of rain falls annually along the upper Texas coast, and the influx of nutrient-rich fresh water supports lush saltwater marshes and large oyster reefs. Vegetation is abundant and tends to minimize the influence of eolian (wind-related) processes. In South Texas, more arid conditions produce coastal waters with abnormally high salt content, and marshes constitute only a minor bay-margin environment. Instead, windswept tidal flats and large active dune fields dominate the near-shore landscape.

The inland limit of the northern Gulf Coastal Plain is topographically unremarkable, but its western margin is abruptly marked in Central and South Texas by the Balcones Escarpment. Annual average precipitation across this inland part of the Gulf Coastal Plain slips from a soggy 50 inches in the bayous near the Sabine River to about 30 inches in the Austin-San Antonio area and ultimately shrivels to 20 inches at Del Rio. Forests thrive in the northern half of the Texas Gulf Coast. They include pine, oak, ash, and hickory forests in East Texas, and gum, oak, magnolia, pecan, and thickets of palmetto near the Sabine River. Southwestward, the forests thin and finally yield to the mesquite, cactus, and dry-soil grasses of the South Texas brush country.

Black and Grand Prairies

The Black and Grand Prairies are found in Northeast Texas, centered roughly on Dallas and forming concentric belts extending southward to the Edwards Plateau (fig. 2.1). There is no distinctive topographic marker between the upper Gulf Coastal Plain and the Black Prairie, but the transition from rocks of Cenozoic to rocks of Cretaceous age produces a noticeable change in soil and vegetation. Limestone and marl underlying the Black Prairie decompose to produce the region's characteristically deep black soil. This lime-rich soil limits the East Texas timbered belt, which prefers the thin, well-drained, red, clay and sandy soils of the Gulf Coastal Plain. Soil of the Black Prairie is easily cultivated, and this region developed early and rapidly as a farming area. Limestone continues to dominate farther westward, under the Grand Prairie, but limestone in the Grand Prairie's more arid environment is more resistant to erosion. The land westward becomes increasingly plateau-like, as rocky limestone ledges become more common, cultivated fields become smaller, and the soil, although still black, thins noticeably.

Edwards Plateau

The Edwards Plateau (fig. 2.1) is underlain by a hard, slightly inclined, Cretaceous limestone layer. The plateau's elevation decreases gradually eastward to the place where it is abruptly separated from the

FIG. 2.4. The eroded eastern edge of the Edwards Plateau exposes limestone layers along Ranch Road 337 west of Medina. Courtesy *Texas Highways.*

Gulf Coastal Plain by the Balcones Escarpment. The escarpment, three hundred miles long, is a dissected limestone wall trending southwest from Waco to San Antonio, then curving westward and losing definition near Del Rio at the Mexico border. The escarpment formed in the geologic past from movement along a crustal break known as the Balcones Fault zone. Some geologists believe that Central Texas was uplifted about ten to twenty million years ago (Miocene time) as part of the regional uplift of all of western North America. Others argue that regional uplift occurred earlier, and that later Miocene movement along the Balcones fault zone dropped the coastal-plain side downward in a stepwise fashion. Viewed from the east, hills with flat tops rise upward across the fault zone in a tiered fashion, similar to balconies, or *balcones,* as the early Spanish explorers called them.

Erosion has caused the Balcones Escarpment to be removed locally inland somewhat from the actual fault zone. In places the plateau surface has been deeply cut by streams such as the Nueces, Frio, Medina, Guadalupe, and Blanco (fig. 2.4). Countless caves (see chapter 8) underlie the limestone plateau, and the upper reaches of many of the streams end in steep-walled box canyons fed by springs from underground rivers. The eastern part of the plateau can be heavily forested with oak, cedar, and mesquite; and valleys there may be lined with large deciduous trees. Westward, as precipitation decreases, trees become increasingly stunted and less numerous.

The cultural influence of the escarpment has been enormous. Timber and stone from the uplifted side of the fault, rivers draining from the Edwards Plateau, and springs issuing from faults at the base of the escarpment have provided conditions for the location of such towns as Austin, San Marcos, New Braunfels, and San Antonio. The escarpment virtually forms a line in the limestone between the cotton-sorghum farming culture of the Old South and the ranch lands of the Old West.

North-Central Plains

Cretaceous rocks, like those exposed in the Grand Prairie and Edwards Plateau, long ago were removed by erosion from the North-Central Plains (fig. 2.1). The surface there is one of variable relief, depending on the resistance to erosion of the underlying Paleozoic formations. To the north, gently dipping Paleozoic rocks form what is commonly called the "Rolling Plains." Geologically they form something of a mirror image of the younger Gulf Coastal Plain rocks. While rock beneath the Coastal Plain dips and becomes younger to the east, strata underlying the North-Central Plains dip and form progressively younger sedimentary layers westward. Just as Cenozoic sediments are beginning to fill the Gulf, these formations represent the progressive filling of a late Paleozoic marine basin in West Texas. That sediment was carried westward in streams draining the ancient Ouachita Mountain range that once towered where the prairies around Dallas now lie.

Central Mineral Region

Southward, in the Central Mineral Region (also known as the Llano area), billion-year-old Precambrian granite and metamorphic rocks poke through the younger Paleozoic and Mesozoic cover. Although granite is a hard rock, in the semi-arid Central Texas climate it is less resistant to erosion than limestone. As a result, the Central Mineral Region forms a basin floored by metamorphic rock and granite and rimmed by Paleozoic and Cretaceous limestone formations of the North-Central Plains and the Edwards Plateau. The basin floor is studded with what

Fɪɢ. 2.5. Enchanted Rock is a homogeneous dome-shaped mass of granite 1.1 billion years old. The granite is exposed at Enchanted Rock State Park in the Central Mineral Region. Courtesy *Texas Highways.*

locally are called mountains, impassive granite domes or ridges of Paleozoic limestone rising to heights of 400 to 600 feet (fig. 2.5).

Southern High Plains

The Southern High Plains, or Llano Estacado (yá-no es-ta-cáh-do), is the southward continuation of the Great Plains Province (fig. 2.1). The term Llano Estacado is in common use. Its name means staked plain, but the origin of the term has been lost. Some books say that Coronado had to stake his route across the High Plains in order to retrace his steps, while others contend that his men had to tether their horses to stakes in this landscape devoid of trees. Still other authors think the stakes refer to the palisaded appearance of the High Plains' caprock, as viewed along the eastern edge of the plateau. I've also heard that the stakes refer to the lechuguilla stalks rising from the High Plains' flat surface, but my personal favorite explanation is that the term should actually be "steaked plain," since the area produces more cattle than any other region of the state.

The Southern High Plains look perfectly flat, but actually they have a slight southeastward tilt. The surface is well under 3,000 feet above sea level in the Midland area, but northwestward it rises imperceptibly to an elevation of about 4,000 feet at the northwestern corner of the Panhandle. The rise toward the Rockies reflects the province's origin in sediment shed from that Rocky Mountain source. Tilted or not, the province is about as flat as a land surface can get. Names such as Plains, Plainview, and Levelland and a host of jokes tell it all. (They say, for example, that you can see Amarillo from Midland if you stand on the hood of your car.)

It was uplift of the Rocky Mountains (Laramide orogeny) during late Cretaceous and early Cenozoic time that caused the first sedimentary layers to be deposited across the High Plains. These rocks, however, were in the process of being removed by stream erosion when renewed uplift deposited the Ogallala Formation. As the climate became arid, thick eolian sand and silt covered earlier stream deposits, and a caliche cap developed on the Ogallala. Fossils of the saber-toothed cats, mastodons, rhinoceroses, horses, camels, and tortoises preserved in the Ogallala strata tell of a time when the High Plains must have looked somewhat like the plains of Africa.

The province is now separated from the Great Plains to the north by the Canadian River (fig. 2.1), which drains from the Rocky Mountains. The Canadian River Valley is located in a long, low trough resulting from subsidence following the dissolution of salt from the underlying late Paleozoic (Permian period) strata. Canadian River water entering Lake Meredith contains 0.3 percent dissolved salt, about one-tenth the salinity of sea water. During the Ice Age (Pleistocene), when rainfall was high, the Canadian River cut an impressive canyon across the northern Panhandle to form the colorful "breaks" country. Further south, tributaries of the Red River have carved spectacular Palo Duro Canyon and the cliffs seen at Caprock Canyons State Park. The brilliant red shales and sandstones exposed in Palo Duro Canyon and other tributary canyons of the Red River provide the sediment that occasionally makes that border river run red. The Eastern Caprock Escarpment, as it is known, divides the High Plains from the Rolling Plains portion of the North-Central Plains. Running roughly two hundred miles north-south from Amarillo to Interstate Highway 20 near Big Spring, this escarpment is the result of erosion by tributaries to the Colorado, Brazos, and the Red rivers (Matthews 1983). Southward, however, the gravel mantle of the High Plains yields inconspicuously to the limestone terrain of the Edwards Plateau.

FIG. 2.6. Some typical Southern High Plains "scenery," complete with playa lake. Courtesy *Texas Highways.*

Probably the most conspicuous geomorphic features of the High Plains are the numerous small ephemeral lakes called *playas* (fig. 2.6). More than thirty thousand of these circular depressions dot the surface of the plains. Most are less than half a mile in diameter, but there are more than forty of considerable size. Eolian processes are important on the High Plains, and many playas have lee-side dunes of wind-blown lake-bed sediment on their east and southeast sides.

Sand dunes are particularly abundant below the Western Caprock Escarpment, along the southwestern side of the High Plains. Outstanding examples can be seen in Monahans Sandhills State Park (fig. 2.7) (Machenberg 1984). A visitor there is treated to a scene straight out of Saudi Arabia. Pumping oil wells nestle between towering, active dunes. West of the dune field lies the valley of the Pecos River. It separates the High Plains province from the mountains and basins of Trans-Pecos Texas, and it serves as the sediment source for Monahans' dunes.

The sand dunes began to form only a few thousand years ago, as the Ice Age ended and aridity began to grip the area. The drier climate re-

FIG. 2.7. Active sand dunes at Monahans Sandhills State Park.
Courtesy *Texas Highways.*

duced the once-mighty Pecos River to its present trickle and thinned the vegetation along its floodplain, exposing sediment to those active West Texas winds. The yearly average rainfall is now only 12 inches, and the region periodically is subjected to severe droughts. When the wind exceeds approximately 14 miles per hour, sand grains begin to move along in small jumps (saltating). Over the past few thousand years, strong westerly winds have blown sand into dunes up to 85 feet high. The dunes migrate slowly eastward until they encounter and are blocked by the Western Caprock Escarpment. There, the frustrated dunes are continually falling apart, only to rise again with gritty determination for yet another assault on the escarpment.

The sand displays a variety of common dune types, including small dunes formed in the wind-shadows of vegetation clumps, isolated barchan dunes, parabolic dunes, and large wavelike transverse dunes. The sand is fine and very pure, consisting of 98 percent of quartz grains and only 2 percent of other minerals and rock fragments. Surprisingly, in this stark landscape, small marshes are found between the towering dunes. For millennia they have been a welcome source of water. Artifacts

FIG. 2.8. Typical Basin-and-Range topography, as seen from the Chisos Mountains of Big Bend National Park. Courtesy *Texas Highways*.

occasionally found following dune migration, such as flint chips, charred hearthstones, and broken animal bones, attest to human occupation here as early as ten thousand years ago.

Trans-Pecos Texas

For many, Trans-Pecos Texas is our state's most interesting physiographic province; certainly it is the most diverse. Texas west of the Pecos is an eclectic blend of mountains, plateaus, and plains, overlying an equally varied geological base. Modest exposures of ancient Precambrian rocks are encountered near Van Horn and El Paso, and Paleozoic sedimentary rocks are found in some abundance. Younger Mesozoic marine sedimentary rocks are very abundant, as are Cenozoic sedimentary and volcanic rocks. Much of the region consists of north-south elongated, fault-bound basins and ranges akin to those found throughout the Basin and Range Province from West Texas to the California border (fig. 2.8). These include the Guadalupe Range, with Guadalupe Peak (fig. 2.9) forming the highest point in Texas (8,751 feet above sea level).

FIG. 2.9. The craggy face of El Capitán, with Guadalupe Peak above and behind. Courtesy *Texas Highways.*

The Guadalupe Mountains are composed of late Paleozoic (Permian) limestone, and they are but a small exposed part of the Capitan Reef. Some consider this reef to be one of the largest fossil reefs in the world, while others believe it to be an enormous bank of fossil skeletal debris. Reef, bank, or both, Capitan abounds in fossil sponges, algae, and bryozoians; and it formed in Late Paleozoic time around what is known as the Delaware Basin, the western part of the even larger Permian Basin.

Guadalupe Peak is only slightly higher than Mount Livermore (8,382 feet), the highest peak in the Davis Mountains of central Trans-Pecos Texas. Mount Livermore, however, is composed of volcanic rock, and the Davis Mountains contain the largest continuous exposures of volcanic rock in Trans-Pecos Texas. Recent dating suggests this enormous pile of volcanic rock was put in place during a relatively short period (about 1.5 million years) of intense volcanic activity approximately 37 million years ago (Mid-Cenozoic time).

Much of southern Trans-Pecos Texas lies in Big Bend, a national park established in 1944. The park's first superintendent, Ross Maxwell, relates

FIG. 2.10. The Rio Grande
River cuts through Maris-
cal Canyon at Big Bend
National Park.
Courtesy *Texas Highways.*

(Maxwell 1968) the Indian legend of how Big Bend was made by the
Great Spirit from material left after making the stars, the rest of the
Earth, and all living things. The Indians, then, recognized and appre-
ciated the region's great biologic and physiographic diversity. Deformed
Paleozoic rocks are found at the northern end of the Big Bend National
Park, and folded and faulted Mesozoic sedimentary rocks are magnifi-
cently exposed for over one hundred miles along the Rio Grande, as it
cuts through spectacular Santa Elena, Mariscal, and Boquillas canyons
(fig. 2.10). Cenozoic sedimentary and volcanic rocks also are abundant at
places like the Chisos Mountains in the heart of Big Bend Park.

Big Bend Ranch, a recently designated state natural area just west of
the national park, is "cut from the same cloth." Big Bend Ranch includes
the Solitario, a remarkable circular uplift that exposes more than 500
million years of Big Bend geologic history. Major episodes include (1) the
depositing of Paleozoic sedimentary rocks, (2) Ouachita Mountain building at the end of Paleozoic time, (3) depositing of Cretaceous limestone

and shale, (4) Rocky Mountain folding and faulting, (5) Mid-Cenozoic volcanic activity, and (6) faulting that continues to the present day.

References

Machenberg, Marcie, D. 1984. *Geology of Monahans Sandhills State Park, Texas.* Guidebook 21. Austin: Bureau of Economic Geology, University of Texas at Austin. 39p.

Matthews, William H., III. 1983. *The geologic story of Palo Duro Canyon.* Guidebook 8. Austin: Bureau of Economic Geology, University of Texas at Austin. 51p.

Maxwell, Ross A. 1968. *The Big Bend of the Rio Grande: A guide to the rocks, landscape, geologic history, and settlers of the area of the Big Bend National Park.* Guidebook 7. Austin: Bureau of Economic Geology, University of Texas at Austin. 138p.

———, with contributions from L. Brown, G. Eifler, and L. Garner. 1970. *Geologic and historic guide to the state parks of Texas.* Guidebook 10. Austin: Bureau of Economic Geology, University of Texas at Austin. 197p.

Morton, Robert. 1988. Late Quaternary geology of the Texas Coastal Plain. In *GSA centennial field guide,* edited by O. T. Hayward, 4:445–58. Boulder, Colo.: South-Central Section, Geological Society of America.

Weise, Bonnie R., and W. A. White. 1980. *Padre Island National Seashore: A guide to the geology, natural environments and history of a Texas barrier island.* Guidebook 17. Austin: Bureau of Economic Geology, University of Texas at Austin. 94p.

3 Texas Weather and Climate

Vexed sailors curse the rain
for which poor shepherds prayed in vain.
—Edmond Waller (English poet, 1606–1687)

Texas has blistering heat and blue northers, dusters and deluges, hail and hurricanes, tornadoes and an occasional temperate autumn day. From marine coasts to mountain crests, plains to plateaus, deltas to deserts, no other state has such a wide spectrum of climatic conditions. If you don't like Texas weather, the saying goes, just stick around and it will change. *Texas Weather* (Bomar 1983) is an excellent popular book on the subject, and the *Texas Almanac* supplies a good summary of each past year's climatic conditions, as well as weather highlights from previous years.

The information upon which these climatic communications is based comes from the National Weather Service. The service monitors surface conditions at nearly two dozen Texas stations and keeps tabs on the upper atmosphere with instruments borne aloft by helium-filled balloons launched twice daily from eight Texas sites. In addition, Texas skies are scanned by radar stations located throughout the state. The weather service recently reorganized its Texas offices and installed a powerful doppler radar system. The doppler radar has about a thousand times the sensitivity of instruments used in the old radar network and so supplies much more accurate information when severe weather threatens. Moreover, the Cooperative Weather Observer Network consists of a small army of private citizens who faithfully record daily precipitation and temperature extremes. Each month these folks submit their observations to the National Weather Service. With the cooperation of this meteorological mob, Texas has at least one climatological data station in every county and more than six hundred statewide. From this deluge of data, general climatic patterns on Texas temperature, rainfall, and wind have been identified.

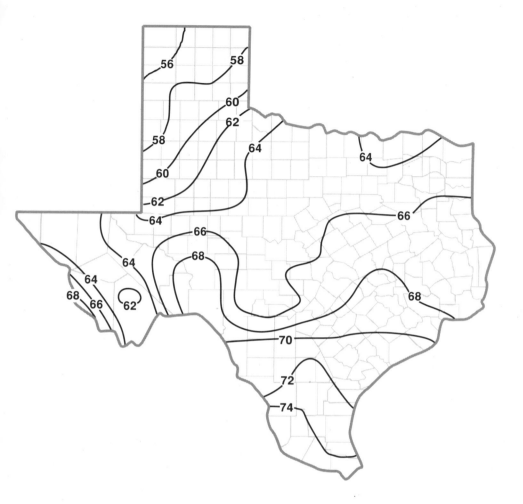

Fig. 3.1. Mean annual temperature across Texas, in degrees Fahrenheit.
Map by Nancy Place; adapted from Kier et al. (1977).

The General Climatic Pattern
Temperatures

Average temperature zones (fig. 3.1) generally, as one might expect, run east and west, parallel to lines of latitude. On any given day, the state's or even the nation's highest temperature commonly is

registered in the Rio Grande River Valley, often at Presidio. The highest
Texas temperature ever recorded, however, was reached at Seymour,
sixty miles southwest of Wichita Falls, on August 12, 1936—a blistering 120 degrees Fahrenheit. (The highest temperature recorded in the
United States was 134 degrees Fahrenheit, reached on July 10, 1913, at
Greenland Ranch in California's Death Valley. The world record is 136
degrees Fahrenheit, recorded in Libya.)

Seminole, fifty miles north of Midland-Odessa, and Tulia, a bit farther
north, share the low temperature record of –23 degrees Fahrenheit, recorded on February 8, 1933 (Seminole), and February 12, 1899 (Tulia).
That 1899 cold wave set records across the state, pushing temperatures
at Galveston as low as 7.5 degrees Fahrenheit and causing a thin layer of
ice to form over most of Galveston Bay.

Rainfall

Texas is considered a semiarid state because more than half of
Texas receives less than thirty inches of precipitation per year. General-
izations about a state with ten climatic divisions, however, are not very
helpful. Texas extends from the humid American South to the arid
American Southwest, and average annual precipitation decreases
westward across the state at the fairly consistent rate of an inch for every
fifteen miles. Lines of average annual precipitation run north and south
(fig. 3.2), directly perpendicular to the thermal contours. Average annual rainfall across the state ranges from over 56 inches in the lower
Sabine River Valley of extreme East Texas to less than 8 inches at El
Paso. It rains an average of about 150 days per year in the Sabine River
Valley, while there are usually only 40 to 50 "rain days" a year in Trans-
Pecos Texas. Trans-Pecos Texas also holds the record for least annual
rainfall. Parched Presidio received a scant 1.64 inches during all of 1956.
Clarksville, sixty miles west of Texarkana, boasts the record for high
annual rainfall. In 1873, this East Texas town received 109.38 inches.
That's over nine feet of rain!

A hurricane entering Mexico in September 1921 caused the single
greatest rainstorm in Texas history. Torrential rains pounded the Balcones Escarpment, as moisture-laden Gulf air was deflected upward into
towering thunderclouds. The U.S. Weather Bureau station at Taylor,
just north of Austin, received 23.98 inches of rain during a period of
35 hours, 23.11 inches of that rain falling during one 24-hour period.
Thrall, an unofficial site nearby, in just 18 hours received 36.40 inches,

FIG. 3.2. Mean annual precipitation across Texas, in inches.
Map by Nancy Place; adapted from Bomar (1983).

the greatest rainfall ever recorded in U.S. history. Floods from the storm killed 215 persons throughout Texas, and five to nine feet of water stood in downtown San Antonio. During August 1–4, 1978, the remnants of tropical storm Amelia dumped more than 48 inches of rain near the Central Texas town of Medina, establishing a new U.S. record for rainfall during a 72-hour period. Other rainfall totals of note are listed in table 3.1.

Table 3.1   Some Amazing Texas 24-Hour Rainfall Totals*

City	Location	Total Inches	Date
Albany	North-Central Plains	29.05	4 Aug. 1978
Alvin	Gulf Coast	25.75	26 Jul. 1979
Danevang	Gulf Coast	20.60	27–28 Aug. 1945
Deweyville	Gulf Coast	20.60	18 Sept. 1963
Freeport	Gulf Coast	16.72	26 Jul. 1979
Kaffie Ranch	South Texas	21.02	12 Sept. 1971
Montel	South Texas	20.60	27 Jun. 1913
Benavides	South Texas	19.20	11 Sept. 1971
Fort Clark	South Texas	18.00	14–15 Jun. 1899
Taylor	Central Texas	23.11	9–10 Sept. 1921
Hye	Central Texas	20.70	11 Sept. 1952
Austin	Central Texas	19.03	9–10 Sept. 1921
Blanco	Central Texas	17.43	11 Sept. 1952

Source: Bomar, *Texas Weather* (1983)

*Does not include the unofficial 24-hour total of 38 inches reported near Thrall in the great storm of 9–10 Sept. 1921.

Trans-Pecos Texas presents the most obvious exceptions to the east-to-west increase in aridity. Mountain "rainfall oases" are created there as the passing atmosphere is uplifted, cooled, and drained of its moisture. The "bull's-eye" patterns on figure 3.2 are located around the Davis Mountains north of Alpine and the Chisos Mountains in Big Bend National Park. Other mountains also must experience increased precipitation, but there are no gauging stations there to record precipitation.

A less obvious exception to the westward increase in aridity is indicated by the slight westward deflection of contour lines along the Balcones Escarpment, a fairly abrupt 1,000-foot increase in elevation between the Gulf Coastal Plain and the Edwards Plateau. Kerrville, for example, fifty miles northwest of San Antonio via Interstate Highway 10, would be expected to receive about 3 inches less rain annually than does the Alamo City. Yet Kerrville actually has a slightly higher average annual precipitation (29.97 versus 29.13 inches).

Another fifty miles west brings us to Junction, where the annual rainfall rate (22.52 inches) is almost seven inches less than that of San Antonio, just as the overall precipitation pattern would predict.

Spring is the wettest season of the year over most of Texas. In Trans-Pecos Texas and the High Plains, however, rain is most plentiful in the summer. Much of the eastern half of Texas, including Dallas, Houston, and San Antonio, have both spring and early fall rainfall peaks. The higher than average September amounts reflect the influence of tropical weather systems that tend to move in from the Gulf of Mexico at that time of year.

Wind and Dust

Virtually all of Texas is under the influence of a southerly wind during July and August. Winter, however, brings a succession of arctic air masses with potent northerly winds commonly called "blue northers." Spring tends to be windy all across Texas, but if they gave awards for bluster, the High Plains would breeze to victory. During spring, the Texas High Plains is one of the windiest regions in all of North America.

"Does the wind blow this way here all the time?" asks the stranger in the old joke. "No, mister," drawls the cowboy, "it will maybe blow this way for a week or ten days; then it'll take a change and blow like hell for awhile." From March through May, the wind's velocity averages from 13 to 17 mph, with periodic episodes during which the air accelerates to two or three times that speed and gusts to 60, 70, or even 80 mph.

Associated with these winds at times are the legendary Texas dusters. In March, 1977, for example, surface winds of 75 to 80 mph reduced visibility at Amarillo to 0.5 mile for ten hours. When the dust settled, much of the Panhandle winter wheat crop had been lost. In 1971, a gigantic March duster reduced visibility to less than a mile at Dallas and to barely over a mile as far south as Brownsville.

The Texas High Plains also endure prolonged periodic droughts, like the one that persisted from 1935 to 1939 (fig. 3.3). Known as the "Dust Bowl Days" or "Dirty Thirties," drought gripped the Panhandle hard but spared much of the rest of Texas. Thousands of High Plains range animals died of starvation or were suffocated by dust. Another extremely dry period of extensive wind erosion took place in 1954–57, when drought affected virtually all of Texas.

Climatic Divisions of Texas

Texas is divided into ten climatic divisions (Griffiths 1987), considered here in a general east-to-west sequence (fig. 3.4). The climatic

Fɪɢ. 3.3 Dry land farming at its worst, during the Dust Bowl Days in the Texas Panhandle, 1938. Photo by U.S. Department of Agriculture; courtesy U.S. National Oceanic and Atmospheric Administration.

divisions have much in common with the ten Texas physiographic provinces of the previous chapter, reflecting the intimate relationship between landforms and climate.

Texas Gulf Coast

The Texas Gulf Coast is divided into the Upper, South-Central, and Lower Valley divisions (fig. 3.4). The Upper Coast Division extends from the Louisiana border southwest to Victoria and Port O'Connor. The region is usually classified as humid subtropical with warm summers. The division's climate is generally controlled by its proximity to the Gulf, but during winter, all the coastal divisions can be affected by strong polar air masses. The Upper Coast has a small annual temperature range and a bimodal seasonal rainfall pattern with both summer and winter peaks. Annual precipitation averages about 48 inches, ranging from 56

FIG. 3.4. Climactic divisions of Texas.
Map by Nancy Place; adapted from Griffiths (1987).

inches near Beaumont to about 37 inches at Victoria. The division is subject to occasional tropical disturbances that can produce 24-hour rainfall
totals of 10 inches or more.

The South-Central Division, centered on Corpus Christi, generally is
designated as humid subtropical with hot summers. Again, the climate

is determined largely by the adjacent Gulf of Mexico, but average annual precipitation here drops to 32 inches, and ranges from about 42 inches near the coast to 26 inches inland. Slight precipitation peaks occur in May and September.

The Lower Valley, in the McAllen-Harlingen-Brownsville area, is the smallest of the ten divisions. It is on the delta of the Rio Grande, just above sea level, and is classified as semiarid subtropical with warm or hot summers. Although it is adjacent to the Gulf and its relative humidity is high, the relatively low annual rainfall averages only 19 to 27 inches. Hurricanes, however, can bring intense rainfall in the summer and early fall. Few really cold Canadian air masses make it as far as the Lower Valley, but temperatures do plummet occasionally to the low twenties or the teens, destroying citrus and other winter crops.

East and North-Central Divisions

The East Division, centered on Tyler (fig. 3.4), usually is designated as humid subtropical with hot summers. Its average annual rainfall total of around 45 inches reflects a westward decrease in precipitation, from 55 inches along the Sabine River Valley (fig. 3.5) to about 40 inches at the border with the North-Central Division. In general, seasonal rainfall is quite uniform, although May, on average, is the wettest month. Summers tend to be hot and humid.

The North-Central Division, centered on the Dallas-Fort Worth area (fig. 3.4), is the state's second largest division. It is classified as subtropical with dry winters and hot, humid summers, and the division has a bimodal precipitation pattern with May and September rainfall maximums. The September maximum is the result of hurricanes and tropical storms that migrate out of the Gulf of Mexico in the early fall. The regional mean precipitation of 32 inches reflects a progressive decrease from about 40 inches in the east to about 25 inches in the west.

Edwards Plateau and Southern Divisions

In general, the Edwards Plateau (fig. 3.4) is described as subtropical steppe with low summer humidity. The mean annual precipitation on the plateau ranges from about 30 inches along the Balcones Escarpment to only 14 inches along the Pecos River (fig. 3.6).

The Southern Division (fig. 3.4) lies south of the Edwards Plateau along the Rio Grande from Eagle Pass almost to McAllen. It is classified as subtropical with warm or hot summers. Its rainfall averages are lower

Fɪɢ. 3.5. An average annual precipitation of about fifty inches nurtures swamps and cypress trees on Village Creek in the Big Thicket.
Courtesy *Texas Highways.*

than nearby coastal divisions, ranging from about 28 inches in the east to 18 inches in the west. Generally the region is influenced by the Gulf of Mexico, and tropical disturbances can bring months with more than 10 inches of rain. ·

Low Rolling Plains and High Plains

The Low Rolling Plains (fig. 3.4), from Abilene north to the Red River, corresponds largely to the North-Central Plains physiographic province. It is similar in many ways to the High Plains Division, but its lower elevation reduces annual temperature extremes. Even so, the division has the single highest recorded temperature (120 degrees Fahrenheit) in Texas. The average annual precipitation is 23 inches, and the area is classified as warm-temperate steppe. The northern part of the division lies in the infamous "Tornado Alley," an area subject to violent thunderstorms.

The High Plains Division, centered on Lubbock (fig. 3.4), is the largest and most northerly climatic division in Texas. It is classified as

FIG. 3.6. An average annual precipitation of about fourteen inches
supports little vegetative cover at the southern margin of the Edwards
Plateau, where U.S. Highway 90 crosses the Pecos River east of Langtry.
Courtesy *Texas Highways.*

a dry steppelike climate and has an average annual precipitation of
about 18 inches. Rainfall rates decrease across the division, from about
22 inches in the east to only 12 inches in the west. Winters tend to be
dry, with about 80 percent of the precipitation coming in the six
months from April to October. Winds are mainly from the south and
southwest, but a northerly flow often dominates during the winter
months, when rapidly moving polar air masses sweep southward, producing dramatic temperature drops. Spring is the windiest season;
and dry winter weather, followed by persistently high, westerly spring
winds, can produce atmospheric dust that drastically reduces visibility. The High Plains Division has the lowest average annual temperature and holds the record low recorded temperature (−23 degrees
Fahrenheit). Most summer days exceed 90 degrees, but the high average elevation and low humidity make summer evenings comfortably
cool.

FIG. 3.7. A typical tornado. This twister struck Novelty, Missouri, on April 21, 1967. Courtesy U.S. National Oceanic and Atmospheric Administration.

Trans-Pecos Division

Trans-Pecos (fig. 3.4) is the most mountainous division, and the fragmented nature of its terrain is reflected in large local climatic variations. Elevations below about four thousand feet above sea level tend to be arid and subtropical; higher altitudes are classified as cool-temperate-humid with warm summers. Most precipitation comes in the form of summer thundershowers, particularly in mountainous areas. The division's total average annual precipitation is below 12 inches. El Paso, the region's largest and most westerly city, receives average annual precipitation of only 8 inches. Presidio averages over eighty 100-degree days per year, and the Trans-Pecos region holds the record for least amount of annual rainfall (1.64 inches at Presidio in 1956).

Texas Tornadoes

A funnel may hang from a thundercloud like a swirling pendant, but it is not technically a tornado until it touches the ground (fig. 3.7).

Texas—where contrasting air masses from the cold North, the arid West, and the warm Gulf tend to converge—is a natural spawning ground for the intense thunderstorms that generate tornadoes. The story of Texas tornadoes, from the first recorded strike in 1856 to the Lubbock twister of 1970, is graphically told by Dudley Lynch in his book, *Tornado: Texas Demon in the Wind* (1970).

A remarkable average of 118 tornadoes spin across Texas each year, more than any other state receives. Most occur along the Red River Valley—"Tornado Alley," as it is called. In Texas an unlucky average of thirteen deaths per year result, the nation's highest tornado death rate. As Mark Twain observed, however, "There are three kinds of lies; there are lies, damned lies, and statistics." (Statistics show, for example, that the largest town in the largest county in the largest of the lower forty-eight states is Alpine, Texas, whose population is 5,637.) On a tornadoes-per-square-mile basis, Texas ranks eleventh among the states, while Oklahoma ranks first. Still, Texas does receive its share, and the 232 Texas tornadoes recorded in 1967 are still the most ever recorded by a state in a given year. Of these, 115 were associated with Hurricane Beulah—another record, this one for hurricane-related tornadoes. Fortunately, tornadoes associated with hurricanes tend to be small and are inclined to remain on the ground for only a short time.

At the other end of the spectrum are monstrous twisters that may last for hours and leave behind wide swaths of destruction. On April 9, 1947, for example, a tornado cut a 221-mile path from the Texas Panhandle through Oklahoma and into Kansas. As the tornado sped up U.S. Highway 60 through the Panhandle towns of White Deer, Glazier, and Higgins, sixty-eight Texans were killed. The tornado lifted a freight train from its tracks near White Deer and killed sixteen Glazier residents and forty-five citizens of Higgins. The tornado continued on across Oklahoma and into Kansas, claiming 169 victims in all. It persisted an amazing six hours; and at Higgins, the path of destruction was a mile and a half wide, as wide as any ever recorded.

What if one of these fat funnels were to strike a major metropolitan area? One did strike Wichita Falls on April 10, 1979, and the result was devastating indeed (fig. 3.8). The twister destroyed over three thousand homes, left 42 people dead, 1,740 injured, and an estimated 20,000 homeless! Many of the victims died in automobiles hurled like frisbees by the cyclone. The Wichita Falls tornado of 1979 was the most destructive tornado in Texas history but, surprisingly, not the most deadly. On

FIG. 3.8. The Wichita Falls tornado of April 10, 1979, destroyed over three thousand homes, killed forty-two people, and injured nearly two thousand. Courtesy *Wichita Falls Times Record News.*

May 18, 1902, the small South Texas town of Goliad bore the brunt of a large twister. And on May 11, 1953, a tornado tore through the heart of downtown Waco. Each storm claimed 114 lives.

White Deer, Glazier, Higgins, and Goliad are names on a long list of small towns largely destroyed by tornadoes (see table 3.2). A few others are Bellevue (1906), Melissa (1921), Silverton (1957), and Clarendon (1970), all bowling pins in "Tornado Alley." The twister that hit little Saragosa north of the Davis Mountains in 1987 was particularly devastating, because the town's population numbered just 183. Of these, only 32 escaped death or injury, and the town was almost completely destroyed.

Tornadoes tend to be freakish in nature, missing one place and totally destroying another. Straw may be driven through wood, while babies have been found virtually unharmed in the branches of trees. The following story, repeated from George Bomar's fine book *Texas Weather,* perfectly illustrates the erratic nature of tornadoes.

> One of the most bizarre happenings in Texas' colorful weather
> history, an event verified by the U.S. Weather Bureau, took
> place in the northeastern corner of the Texas Panhandle near

Table 3.2 Texas Tornado Hit List

Date	Locations	Deaths
15 May 1896	Sherman and vicinity	76
18 May 1902	Goliad	114
9 April 1919	Northeast Texas	42
13 April 1921	Melissa	12
2 April 1927	Rocksprings, Edwards County and vicinity	74
9 April 1947	Texas Panhandle, Oklahoma, and Kansas	68
11 May 1953	Waco	114
15 May 1957	Silverton	21
18 April 1970	Clarendon	17
11 May 1970	Lubbock	26
10 April 1979	Wichita Falls (42) and Vernon (12)	54
22 May 1987	Saragosa (Reeves County)	30

Sources: Bomar, *Texas Weather* (1983) and *Texas Almanac* (1991)

the town of Higgins in April 1947. The owner of a home in rural Lipscomb County, upon hearing the loud trainlike noise of an approaching twister, opened his front door and was lifted hundreds of feet into the air over the tops of nearby trees. A visitor in the man's home then went to the same front entrance to check on his friend and was also carried high into the air, but on a slightly different course. After a few very anxious moments, both men were lowered to the ground several hundred feet away from where the house had originally stood. Unharmed but understandably shaken, the pair proceeded to try to walk back to the house but the persistent strong wind forced them to crawl. When they ultimately got back to the site of the house, they found nothing but the foundation. Sitting on the floor was a lamp and a couch containing the owner's terrified but unharmed wife and two children. (Bomar 1983)

Hail

Almost any thunderstorm contains some ice. Ice particles smaller than 0.2 inch (5 mm), are known scientifically as *ice pellets*. *Hail* must have a larger diameter, and if particles are larger than 0.8 inch (2 cm), the meteorologist uses the technical term *large hail*. Popular gradations are more imaginative: pea, marble, golf ball, baseball or tennis ball, softball, grapefruit. No basketballs have yet been reported, but stones larger than grapefruit struck San Antonio in May, 1946.

Hailstorms can be incredibly destructive to crops, roofs, and cars. In 1978, a brief spring hailstorm pummeled Texarkana, causing $10 million in damage to homes, businesses, and automobiles. In August, 1979, hail caused an estimated $200 million dollars worth of damage to seven hundred thousand acres of High Plains cotton, corn, and other crops.

No part of Texas is completely safe from hail, but it is most common in the northern half of Texas, from the Black and Grand Prairies and the Edwards Plateau through the North-Central Plains to the High Plains of the Texas Panhandle. Texas, in fact, leads the nation in average annual loss of crops to hail, and hail dents some portion of the High Plains agricultural economy virtually every year.

Normally hail accumulation is light, but in 1970, 18 inches of hail, some particles the size of baseballs, accumulated on FM 294 west of Amarillo. Bumper-deep hail was reported near Henderson in East Texas following a storm in May, 1976. But the crowning blow, so to speak, may have been that baseball-sized hailstone that crashed through a house window in the Central Texas town of Comfort, striking an occupant on the head and knocking her unconscious.

Hurricanes

A hurricane is a gigantic revolving mass of air some ten miles deep and as wide as one thousand miles (fig. 3.9). Hurricane winds must be at least 74 mph, and they spiral in toward a central zone of low atmospheric pressure. Hurricanes commonly are ranked on a five-part scale of disaster potential developed by Herbert Saffir and Robert Simpson. "Force one" hurricanes, for example, have winds of 74–95 mph; they can damage vegetation, unanchored mobile homes, and poorly constructed signs. They are associated with a 4- to 5-foot storm surge, some coastal flooding, and minor damage to coastal structures. "Force five" hurricanes have winds greater than 155 mph, trees are blown down, all signs and mobile homes are destroyed, there is extensive shattering of glass and failure of roofs, storm surges exceed eighteen feet, and there is extensive coastal flooding and damage.

The hurricane season in the Gulf of Mexico extends from June 1

Fig. 3.9. Hurricane Elena churns over the Gulf of Mexico, September 4, 1985. Courtesy NASA.

through November 30, but no recorded hurricane has hit the Texas coast earlier than June 4 or later than October 17. From 1871 to 1984, forty hurricanes have made landfall in Texas (seventeen others came close enough to cause damage), and twenty-six tropical storms crossed the Texas coast. On average, then, about four hurricanes move in somewhere along the coast every decade, or about one every other year. The longest period without a hurricane was between Hurricane Fern in 1971 and Hurricane Allen in 1980. The tracks of major hurricanes affecting Texas from 1901 through 1994 are shown in figure 3.10.

Texan's experience with hurricanes started early (see table 3.3). In the late nineteenth century, Indianola was a prosperous town on the Calhoun County coast between Galveston and Corpus Christi. On September 16, 1875, three-fourths of the town was swept away and 176 lives lost, when a hurricane's storm surge pushed bay water into the low-lying town. After the disaster, the town's citizenry rebuilt. Another hurricane eleven years later (August 19–21, 1886) wiped the town from the map forever.

Hurricanes in Galveston

Galveston has experienced more than its share of hurricanes. Two occurred in the first week of June, 1871, alone. The *Galveston Weekly* ran the following unfair complaint against the newly appointed local storm observer: "They'd better take that old Sergeant Von Hake

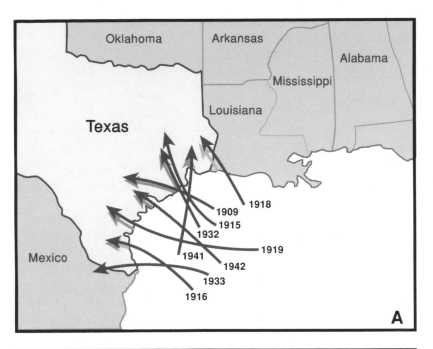

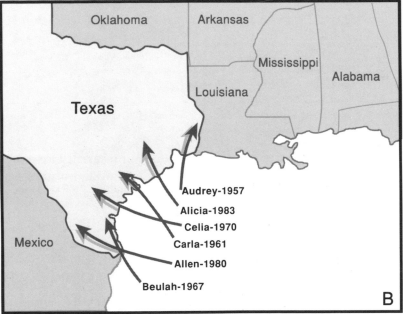

Fig. 3.10. Tracks of category 3 or greater hurricanes affecting Texas in (A) 1901–49 and (B) 1950–93.

Map by Nancy Place; adapted from *Weather Almanac* (1992).

Table 3.3   The Twelve Most Destructive Texas Hurricanes
(in terms of property damage and lives lost)

Date	Location	Maximum Winds (mph)	Notes
16 Sept. 1875	Indianola	?	Town 75% destroyed, 176 deaths
Aug. 1886	Indianola	?	Town destroyed and never rebuilt
8 Sept. 1900	Galveston	125	6,000 to 8,000 deaths, worst natural disaster in U.S. history
17 Aug. 1915	Freeport	120	275 deaths. Seawall saved Galveston
14 Sept. 1919	Corpus Christi	120	284 deaths; $20 million damage
13 Aug. 1932	Freeport	110	40 deaths
4 Sept. 1933	Brownsville	100	40 deaths
11 Sept. 1961	Port O'Connor	150	Carla—largest Texas hurricane. Gusts estimated at 175 mph, 34 deaths, at least $330 million damage
20 Sept. 1967	Brownsville	140	Beulah—Spawned a record 115 tornadoes, 15 deaths
3 Aug. 1970	Corpus Christi	130	Celia—Wind gusts estimate to 180 mph, very extensive wind damage, $453 million damage
10 Aug. 1980	Port Mansfield	115	Allen—Very damaging
18 Aug. 1983	San Luis Pass	115	Alicia—$3 billion damage

Sources: Bomar, *Texas Weather* (1983) and *Texas Almanac* (1991)

away from here. The United States Government just sent him here a couple of weeks ago, and he's done been and brought two storms already. He don't know nothin' about how to manage this here Texas weather."

Sergeant Von Hake likely was gone by September 8, 1900, when Galveston was hit again. Galveston Island and nearby coastal areas were inundated by a storm surge which put water eight to fifteen feet deep in the streets. Rising waters inundated the Galveston Island causeway, destroyed the two bridges, and completely cut the city off from the mainland. The death toll in the Galveston Bay area was at least six thousand

FIG. 3.11. The Galveston seawall was constructed after the disastrous 1900 hurricane that inundated the city and claimed at least six thousand lives in the Galveston Bay area. Photo by author.

and perhaps more than eight thousand. It remains the worst natural disaster in U.S. history, and it is documented in graphic detail by John Weems in his book *A Weekend in September*.

Some of the residents of the island and nearby low coastal areas left and saved themselves. Of those who remained on the island, fewer than one hundred survived. Returning citizens called for action. A seventeen-foot seawall was constructed to protect the city (fig. 3.11), and some 2,156 buildings were elevated to prevent their being flooded. One of the engineers who helped to design the seawall was a stickler for decorum named Henry M. Roberts, who is better remembered for his book *Roberts' Rules of Order*.

Seawall or no, there must have been some nervous moments when a hurricane approached the island in 1915. In fact, the total loss of life for that hurricane is placed at 275, but the enormous loss of life experienced in 1900 never has been repeated. As the years go by, coastal hurricanes seem to claim a decreasing number of casualties. Property damage, however, continues to grow, as the coastal population increases and buildings of all types are placed in harm's way.

Fɪɢ. 3.12. A satellite view of Hurricane Alicia taken during the evening of August 17, 1983, shows the deceptively small hurricane moving toward the Texas coast. Courtesy U.S. National Oceanic and Atmospheric Administration.

Hurricanes Carla and Alicia

Names were not systematically assigned to tropical storms and hurricanes prior to 1954. After that date, hurricanes were given female names, a practice that in 1979 yielded to the nonsexist formula used today. In 1961, the third storm of the season was named Carla. Carla is considered to be the most powerful hurricane to hit Texas in this century. The hurricane's eye measured thirty miles across, and its winds were over 150 mph. Carla came ashore in the Port Lavaca–Port O'Connor area just after noon on September 11, 1961, and churned past the park and monument where Indianola once stood. Warnings of Carla's approach caused a mass exodus, saving many lives. Of those who stayed to play "hurricane roulette," thirty-four lost. Tides were 18.5 feet above normal at Port Lavaca, and winds were estimated at 175 mph. The old causeway running to Port Comfort collapsed, and the fishing resort of Port O'Connor was practically destroyed. Carla removed much of the sand from in front of the Galveston seawall, but the wall survived. Chan-

FIG. 3.13. Pushed by Hurricane Alicia, an eight- to ten-foot storm surge stripped vegetation and removed five feet of sand from beneath these beach-front homes in the Brazosport area just south of Galveston Island. Courtesy U.S. National Oceanic and Atmospheric Administration.

nels were carved by the storm through parts of the Matagorda Peninsula, and dunes on Mustang Island were eroded landward by as much as 150 feet. Once inland, Carla's power diminished, but the hurricane's eye scored a direct hit on Austin, and the storm's movement could be traced northward through Texas and all the way to the Great Lakes.

Alicia was the first hurricane of the 1983 season. Alicia hit the nine-county area around Houston, then inhabited by 3.4 million people (fig. 3.12). Total damage and recovery costs were a staggering $3 billion, the costliest Texas hurricane to date (fig. 3.13).

Hurricane Gilbert

Hurricane Gilbert was the most powerful hurricane yet recorded in the Western Hemisphere. Gilbert roared across the Caribbean in September, 1988, with winds of up to 145 miles per hour, and inflicted $8 billion in damage on Jamaica before continuing on, over warm Caribbean waters. Gilbert's winds gusted to over 200 mph, and its eye narrowed as it took aim on Mexico's Yucatan Peninsula. Weakened somewhat by its encounter with Mexico but still a powerhouse, Gilbert entered the Gulf and menaced the entire Texas coast. Many coastal residents were asked to evacuate. Many others needed no official encouragement; they sought shelter, hunkered down, and waited. When forecasters began calling the storm Gilberto, Texas knew it had largely been spared. Gilberto moved westward into the mountains of Mexico on September 16 (Mexico's Independence Day), where its impact on property and flood victims was severe.

What if Gilbert had swept across Texas instead? It has been over thirty years since Carla did just that. What will happen when a hurricane like Gilbert or Carla hits again? Seawalls and modern weather forecasting make it unlikely that the drastic loss of life experienced at Galveston will be repeated, but the building boom of the 1970s and early 1980s and the complacency engendered by the lack of great Texas hurricanes in recent years have set the stage for property damage of enormous proportions.

References

Bomar, George W. 1983. *Texas weather*. Austin: University of Texas Press. 265p.

Dallas Morning News. 1991. *Texas almanac, 1992–93*, ed. M. Kingston. Houston: Gulf Publishing Co. 656p. Address: Box 2608, Houston TX 77252.

Griffiths, J. 1987. Climactic division descriptions. In *The climates of Texas counties*, edited by Lois G. Shrout, 1–17. Austin: Bureau of Business Research, University of Texas at Austin.

Kier, R. S.; L. E. Garner; and L. F. Brown, Jr. 1977. *Land Resources of Texas*. Austin: Bureau of Economic Geology, University of Texas at Austin. 42p., 1 map.

Lynch, Dudley. 1970. *Tornado: Texas demon in the wind*. Waco: Texian Press. 163p.

The weather almanac. 1992. 6th ed. Detroit, Mich.: Gale Research. 855p.

Weems, John E. 1980. *A weekend in September*. College Station: Texas A&M University Press. 180p.

4 A Brief Geologic
History of Texas

> Researchers have already cast much darkness on the subject, and if
> they continue their investigations, we shall soon know nothing at all
> about it.
> —Mark Twain

On the surface of things, it might not appear that Texas has had a very
interesting geologic history. Much of the state consists of flat plains,
prairies, and plateaus unspectacularly underlain by endless layers of
level-lying rocks. But take a look at El Capitán in the Guadalupe Mountains of far West Texas, the highest point in Texas (8,751 feet above sea
level). That rocky remnant of a reef has risen to prominence from lowly
beginnings beneath an ancient Paleozoic sea. The Davis Mountains, now
quiet and serene, were formed by volcanic explosions of unimaginable
fury. For thirty million years now, these mountains and other giant piles
of volcanic rock and rubble have stood west of the Pecos, stubbornly re-
sisting the forces of erosion.

Geologic action, however, certainly has not been limited to Trans-
Pecos Texas. The geologist's eye sees even more spectacular events
beneath the state's flat sedimentary cover. "Hay sierras debajo de los
llanos," says an old New Mexico expression: "There are mountains
below the plains." Under the flat lands, folded, metamorphosed rocks
suggest at least two mountain ranges that, in their day, may have ri-
valed the Alps or even the Himalayas. Texas, in fact, has rocks of every
geologic age (fig. 4.1), evidence of the state's long and spectacular geologic history, consisting of repeated cycles of continental rifting and
convergence.

Popular reviews of the geologic history of Texas are contained in Darwin Spearing's *Roadside Geology of Texas* and in the 1992–93 edition of the
Texas Almanac. The *Geologic Highway Map of Texas* (1973), published by the
American Association of Petroleum Geologists, presents a wealth of easily understandable geologic information. Ewing's *The Tectonic Framework
of Texas* (1991), written to accompany a revised tectonic map of Texas
(Ewing 1990), describes our state's geologic history in terms of plate

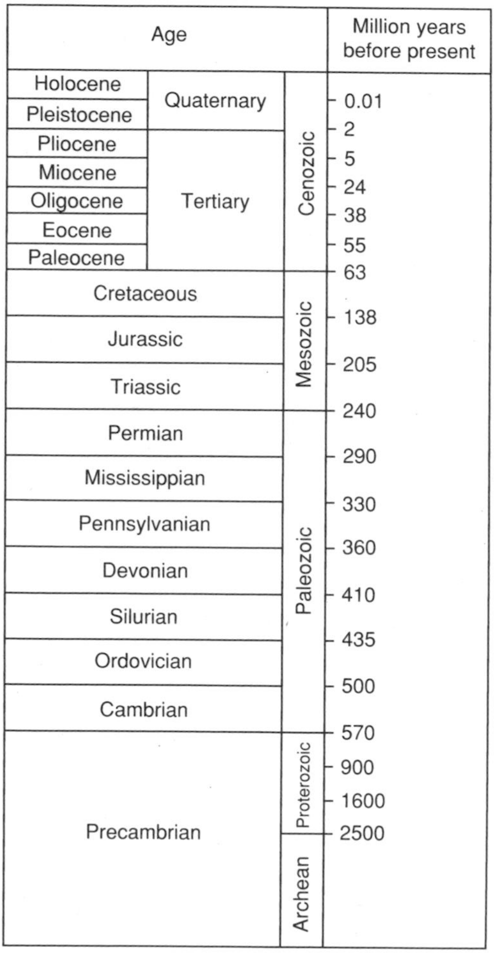

Age			Million years before present
Holocene	Quaternary	Cenozoic	0.01
Pleistocene			2
Pliocene	Tertiary		5
Miocene			24
Oligocene			38
Eocene			55
Paleocene			63
Cretaceous		Mesozoic	138
Jurassic			205
Triassic			240
Permian		Paleozoic	290
Mississippian			330
Pennsylvanian			360
Devonian			410
Silurian			435
Ordovician			500
Cambrian			570
Precambrian	Proterozoic		900
			1600
			2500
	Archean		

FIG. 4.1. Geologic timescale. Chart by Nancy Place.

tectonic cycles that correspond well to Earth's major geologic eras. It is the primary source for the information that follows.

Let me sound two notes of caution. First, despite more than a century of research, it is likely that we know only the basic outline of what actually occurred during the past 1.5 billion years. Second, this chapter portrays 1.5 billion years of Texas geologic history with only three thousand words; that's half a million years per word! Many important events are covered incompletely or not at all.

Precambrian Geologic History of Texas

Sedimentary rocks of the Paleozoic and later eras commonly contain fossils of all descriptions. Precambrian rocks, however, are conspicuously lacking in fossils and typically consist of metamorphosed sedimentary and volcanic rocks pierced by ancient granites. It appears likely that at least two-thirds of Texas lies over igneous and metamorphic rock of Precambrian age (more than 570 million years old). In only three relatively small locations, however, have these layers been uplifted enough to have had their sedimentary veneer removed by erosion (figs. 4.2 and 4.3). The largest exposure of Precambrian rock is in the Central Mineral Region (also known as the Llano area), northwest of Austin in Burnet, Llano, and Mason counties. Smaller Precambrian exposures surface north of El Paso in far West Texas and near Van Horn. Rocks of these three areas are approximately the same age (give or take a hundred million years) and appear to belong to the same ancient mountain chain (the Grenville orogenic belt). These rocks range in age from about 1,300 to 1,070 million years old, yet they are not the oldest Texas rocks. The Grenville belt, in fact, is the youngest Precambrian belt of regional extent in North America, and rocks of the Central Mineral Region mark the approximate location of the southern boundary of Precambrian North America.

In general, the crustal fabric across the southern United States consists of parallel, southwest-trending, rocky belts that become increasingly older away from the Gulf of Mexico. The oldest Texas rocks are expected to underlie the Texas Panhandle. Rock recovered during Panhandle petroleum exploration is reported to be 1.4 billion years old, but even older ages are expected. Rocks exposed in the nearby mountains of northern New Mexico yield ages of up to 1.8 billion years, and geologists expect the oldest Texas rock to be about that age. Ancient though this rock may be, it is but one-third as old as Earth—much younger than the oldest known rock (3.96 billion years, from near Great Slave Lake in northwestern Canada) and the oldest known mineral (a 4.3 billion-year-old zircon grain plucked from a much younger Australian sedimentary rock).

The surface Precambrian rocks of Texas are believed to be small exposed bits of an ancient, eroded mountain chain that can be traced, mostly in the subsurface, all the way to the Grenville area of eastern Canada. Presently it appears that the Grenville mountain belt formed when an ancient continental block, probably Gondwanaland, collided

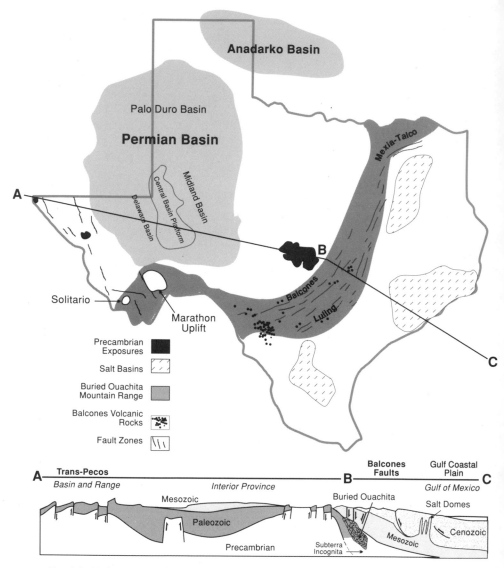

Fɪɢ. 4.2. Major structural elements of Texas and a simplified geologic cross-section. Map by Nancy Place; adapted from AAPG (1973) and Ewing (1990, 1991).

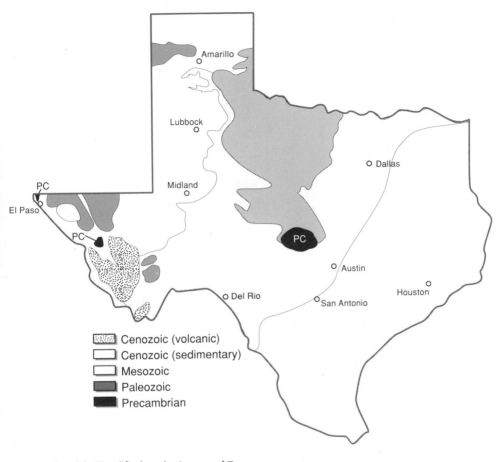

FIG. 4.3. Simplified geologic map of Texas.
Map by Nancy Place; adapted from Kier et al. (1977).

in some complex manner with the southern and eastern margin of North America, sometime between 1.3 and 1.1 billion years ago. The Panhandle Precambrian rocks may record an even earlier continental collision.

Rocks of the Central Mineral Region also record an important igneous event. Roughly half of the area has been pierced by enormous masses of granite dated at slightly over 1 billion years of age. The granite is prominently exposed in the region's distinctive domes, most notably at Enchanted Rock State Park (see fig. 2.4). Enchanted Rock, like most Central Texas granite, consists of a pink, coarse-grained variety called Town Mountain Granite. It is quarried at several locations, including Granite Mountain near Marble Falls. The quarry not only has put a pink glow on the face of downtown Austin, but also it has supplied material for building projects from New York's Grand Central Station to the Los Angeles County Courthouse.

The granite and metamorphic rocks of Central and West Texas are the exposed core of the ancient Grenville range. The overlying Paleozoic sedimentary rocks are only half as old. The sharp contrast between these two sequences represents a half billion years of Earth's history, an enormous time gap for which we have no rock record but erosion.

Paleozoic Geologic History of Texas

At the dawn of the Paleozoic era, about 550 million years ago, North America separated itself from an ancient mystery land mass, and a kind of paleo-Atlantic body of water known as the Iapetus Ocean formed. The rift took place along the southeast side of the Grenville rocks, leaving them attached to Texas and the rest of North America. The continental margin eventually subsided below the shallow margin of the Iapetus Ocean and received a coating of early Paleozoic sandstone, limestone, and shale. These early Paleozoic rocks underlie much of West and North Texas (fig. 4.2), and they are exposed over Precambrian rocks of the Central Mineral Region. They crop out in Trans-Pecos Texas at Van Horn and El Paso (fig. 4.3). Further out in the Paleozoic sea, sediments were also being deposited in the Ouachita Basin, an area of deeper water and the site of the next phase of mountain building. Rare surface exposures of these rocks are now found west of the Pecos in the Marathon and Solitario uplifts (figs. 4.2 and 4.3).

The Iapetus Ocean began closing during the last half of the Paleozoic era (approximately 360 to 245 million years ago), causing crustal compression in Texas. Inland, in West and North Texas, the result was a complex arrangement of uplifts and deep basins collectively known as the Permian Basin (fig. 4.2). Barrier reefs formed around some individual basins, including the late Paleozoic (Permian period) Capitan Reef, now exposed in the Guadalupe Mountains.

As the basins filled and the sea gradually withdrew, the arid Permian climate caused the deposition of an enormous amount of salt and gypsum across parts of West Texas and the Texas Panhandle. These *evaporites*, as they are called, were not the only economically interesting sediment deposited in the basin. Sediment rich in organic material also accumulated there and eventually produced the oil that makes the Permian Basin our nation's largest petroleum province.

Meanwhile, back at the continental edge, the sedimentary formations of the Ouachita Basin, now squeezed by colliding continents, began crumpling up to form the Ouachita Mountain range. The late Paleozoic Ouachita belt is part of a much longer folded and thrust-faulted range that can be traced, mostly in the subsurface, from Mexico to Mississippi and beyond. The belt emerges east of Mississippi as the Southern Appalachian Mountains, a range that in late Paleozoic time was continuous with the folded rocks now found in Europe (Hercynides) and North Africa (Mauritanides). Exposures of Ouachita rocks west of Mississippi are few. They are found, of course, in the folds of the Ouachita Mountains of southwestern Arkansas and southeastern Oklahoma. From there, the belt passes southwestward beneath Dallas, Austin, and San Antonio, to the point where it swings westward to surface again in the Marathon Uplift north of Big Bend National Park, and in the Solitario Uplift just a few miles from the Mexican border (fig. 4.2).

Late Paleozoic Texas differed greatly from today's landscape. At that time, mountains stood high across Texas from Dallas to Del Rio. Late Paleozoic rivers flowed westward, depositing fluvial, deltaic, and shallow marine sediment at a coastline that shifted across North-Central Texas and the Texas Panhandle. Although these rocks subsequently were covered by Mesozoic sediment, uplift and erosion have exposed large areas of late Paleozoic rocks in the North-Central Plains. Along the eastern edge of the Southern High Plains, in places like Caprock Canyons State Park and Palo Duro Canyon, too, brilliantly colored red rocks of Permian age are spectacularly exposed (fig. 4.4).

The Hercynian-Appalachia-Ouachita deformation marked a spectacular end to Paleozoic continental convergence. When it was over, most of Earth's continents had been cobbled together to form the supercontinent of Pangaea, a monster land mass crossed by what must have been a magnificent mountain range. Had these mountains remained, Colorado residents would be spending summer vacations in the mountains of South Texas. Time and the next cycle of rifting, however, removed the Texas mountains and created the Gulf of Mexico.

FIG. 4.4. The lighthouse rock formation at Palo Duro Canyon.
Courtesy *Texas Highways.*

Mesozoic Geologic History of Texas

Somewhat after the beginning of Mesozoic time (in the Triassic period, about 220 million years ago), the supercontinent of Pangaea, from Nova Scotia to southern Mexico, began splitting to form a series of elongated, fault-bound basins. Like Paleozoic rifting before, the Mesozoic split left another foldbelt (Ouachita) attached to North America. By middle Mesozoic time (Jurassic period), the rift basins had widened and subsided to such an extent that the sea entered and began depositing thick layers of salt. Salt deposits are especially thick beneath the Palestine area of East Texas, the Houston-Beaumont area, and a large region south of San Antonio (fig. 4.2).

Although there are ample Triassic and Jurassic rocks in Texas, most have been buried by younger rocks, and surface exposures are rare. In late Jurassic time, the rift system began widening into a small ocean, the Gulf of Mexico. Late Mesozoic time (Cretaceous period) brought a period in which Gulf waters spilled onto the continental margin and over nearly all of Texas. The warm Cretaceous climate promoted the formation of the light-colored, flat-lying limestone formations found in abundance from the Red River north of Dallas, through the Hill Country of Central Texas, to Santa Elena Canyon of the Big Bend of the Rio Grande (fig. 4.3). In places (e.g., Glen Rose), dinosaurs left their tracks and trails in the limy mud flats bordering these shallow coastal waters. In other places, the ground was being prepared for petroleum. In East Texas, for example a fluctuating Cretaceous shoreline was depositing the porous Woodbine Sandstone. After gentle uplift briefly exposed the formation to erosion, it was again submerged and buried beneath an impermeable sedimentary cap. The process created the trap for the giant East Texas oil field (see chapter 7).

All was not completely placid in the warm, shallow, Cretaceous seas, however. The horizon was punctuated here and there by volcanic islands, which, for reasons still not well understood, erupted around the Gulf rim near the end of the Mesozoic era. More than two hundred exposures of Cretaceous igneous rocks are known from volcanic fields around Austin and Uvalde (fig. 4.2). Other igneous rocks of this age are found in Louisiana, Arkansas, and Mississippi. These rocks are of a particularly alkali-rich, silica-poor character which, at its extreme, includes diamond-bearing kimberlite and carbonate igneous rocks in Arkansas. No kimberlite is known from Texas, although one intriguing diamond has been found (see chapter 6)!

During very latest Mesozoic and Early Cenozoic time (about 66 million years ago), the Laramide episode of mountain building was producing the Rocky Mountains in the western United States and the Sierra Madre Oriental in Mexico. Laramide mountain building is related to the interaction between North America and a Pacific Ocean plate known as the Farallon Plate. While Laramide uplift was relatively minor in Texas, it did cause some folding and faulting in Trans-Pecos Texas, and the rising Rockies started sediment-laden streams flowing to the Texas Gulf Coast, where much of the sediment was deposited.

Cenozoic Geologic History of Texas

As sediment accumulated on the subsiding Texas Gulf Coast, the underlying beds of Mesozoic salt began to feel the squeeze. Salt is less dense and much more easily deformed than most other sedimentary rocks, and thick beds of salt began rising in great columns that pierced the overlying sedimentary rock and created domes (fig. 4.2). Structures created by the salt's upward movement made terrific traps for hydrocarbons, traps that filled to form some of the Gulf Coast's incredibly rich oil fields (Spindletop, for example).

Elsewhere, the salt did not rise but served as a weak layer over which sedimentary formations could slowly slide down toward the Gulf. This process is responsible for several major fault zones that parallel the Gulf Coast (fig. 4.2). Some of these faults blocked the migration of hydrocarbons, creating even more Gulf Coast oil fields. The Balcones fault zone, caught between uplift to the west and subsidence of the Gulf, became active and formed the escarpment still seen separating the Edwards Plateau from the Gulf Coastal Plain (fig. 4.2). Gulf Coastal Plain faults still are slightly seismically active. Occasionally they produce a small earthquake (see chapter 5), but mostly they allow rock to creep slowly and silently down toward the Texas coast.

Economically important amounts of sulfur, lignite, and several metals are found piercing or interbedded with Cenozoic rocks of the Gulf Coastal Plain (see chapter 7). Thick sulfur deposits were formed from anaerobic bacterial activity on both the petroleum and anhydrite (calcium sulfate) layers associated with Gulf Coast salt domes. Lignite, a low-grade coal, originated when vegetation along the Cenozoic coastal deltas and lagoons was buried and transformed to coal. Sedimentary processes also produced uranium and iron ores in rocks of the Gulf Coastal Plain. Meanwhile, in Trans-Pecos Texas, thermal waters were depositing veins of silver, mercury, and even a little gold.

Trans-Pecos Texas was the site of some spectacular Cenozoic surface geologic activity. By mid-Cenozoic time, the Farallon Plate's continued thrusting under western North America had given rise to roaring volcanoes. Sporadic magmatism started about 48 million years ago and peaked between 38 and 32 million years ago, when compressional forces applied by the Farallon Plate actually were on the wane. This easing of crustal compression is believed to have permitted large pools of magma to rise and reach the surface in spectacular volcanic eruptions. Great volcanic piles were built up around at least fourteen major eruptive centers. The largest exposure of volcanic rocks is located in central Trans-Pecos Texas, in and around the Davis Mountains (fig. 4.5). Many other Trans-Pecos mountain ranges also wear volcanic caps, and excellent exposures are seen throughout Big Bend National Park (fig. 4.3). Most metal-bearing veins found in Trans-Pecos Texas probably are related to thermal waters heated by these rising Cenozoic magmas. Some, however, may have

FIG. 4.5. Columnar jointed, Cenozoic volcanic rock (Sleeping Lion Formation) above old Fort Davis in the Davis Mountains.
Courtesy *Texas Highways.*

been deposited from water heated by deep circulation along the fault systems that formed somewhat later.

By 24 million years ago, tensional forces had completely replaced compression. The crust was pulled apart, producing widespread faulting in West Texas and allowing the denser basaltic lavas to reach the surface. The faulting formed a series of northwest-trending basins and ranges, and it continues on a modest scale even today. Volcanic activity, on the other hand, appears to have ceased long ago. Still, recent volcanism within miles of the border suggests that future Texas volcanic eruptions are possible.

The western half of the Texas Panhandle or Southern High Plains is covered and capped by late Cenozoic sediment shed from the Rocky Mountains (fig. 4.3). Much of this sediment is found in the Ogallala Formation, the main aquifer for the Southern High Plains. Today, however, the High Plains are rather isolated. As the Rio Grande and Pecos River valleys developed, they intercepted sediment shed to the High Plains and, together with other Texas rivers, they began to gnaw away at the Panhandle caprock. The process was accelerated during the Ice Age

Fıɢ. 4.6. Aerial view of South Padre Island, a typical Texas barrier island. Courtesy *Texas Highways.*

(Pleistocene), when a wetter climate produced a greater flow of water and the Gulf shoreline, because of water frozen in the large polar ice caps, was several hundred feet lower than it is today. The dramatic results of this period of intense erosion can be seen along the so-called "breaks" of the Canadian River, in the width of the Pecos River Valley, and in spectacular Palo Duro Canyon. The sediment eroded from West Texas found its way eastward, feeding deltas growing into the Gulf of Mexico.

As the Pleistocene came to a close, melting polar ice caused a rapid rise in sea level and a shifting of the shoreline to its present position. Texas began to take on a familiar look, as ocean currents reworked the Pleistocene deltas into the lagoons and barrier islands that characterize the modern Texas Gulf Coast (fig. 4.6).

Texas has been the site of repeated cycles of continental rifting and convergence. Things now appear to be fairly quiet, but, from the geologic perspective, Texas is merely enjoying a rather stable period between the cessation of the rifting that formed the Gulf of Mexico and the next compressional phase. The latter probably will uplift, fold, and transform Gulf

Coastal Plain sediments, and crunch them against the older, stable rocks of Central Texas. It may take 100 million years or more for "the South to rise again," but ultimately it will happen. When it does, Beaumont, whose name means beautiful mountain, might become exactly that.

References

The definitive professional works are still volumes 1 and 2 of *The Geology of Texas*. Volume 1, now in its ninth printing, reviews Texas stratigraphy. Volume 2 covers structural and economic geology but is out of print. At nearly a thousand pages long and over sixty years old, however, both volumes are recommended only for professional geologists, historians, and incurable insomniacs.

American Association of Petroleum Geologists. 1973. *Geologic highway map of Texas*. Tulsa, Okla.: American Association of Petroleum Geologists. 1 sheet.

Dallas Morning News, 1991. *Texas almanac, 1992–93*. Edited by M. Kingston. Houston: Gulf Publishing Co. 656p. Address: Box 2608, Houston TX 77252.

Ewing, T. E., comp. 1990. *Tectonic map of Texas*. Austin: Bureau of Economic Geology, University of Texas at Austin. 4 sheets. 1:750,000 scale.

————, 1991. *The tectonic framework of Texas*. Austin: Bureau of Economic Geology, University of Texas at Austin. 36p.

Kier, R. S.; L. E. Garner; and L. F. Brown, Jr. 1977. *Land Resources of Texas*. Austin: Bureau of Economic Geology, University of Texas at Austin. 42p., 1 map.

Sellards, E. H.; W. S. Adkins; and F. B. Plummer. 1932. *The geology of Texas*. Vol. 1: *Stratigraphy*. Bulletin No. 3232. Austin: Bureau of Economic Geology, University of Texas at Austin. 1,007p.

Sellards, E. H., and C. L. Baker. 1934. *The geology of Texas*. Vol. 2: *Structural and economic geology*. Bulletin No. 3401. Austin: Bureau of Economic Geology. University of Texas at Austin. 884p.

Spearing, Darwin R. 1991. *Roadside geology of Texas*. Missoula, Mont.: Mountain Press Publishing Co. 418p. Address: Box 2399, Missoula MT 59806.

5 Texas Volcanoes and Earthquakes

Which would you rather have,
a bursting planet or an earthquake here and there?
—John Lynch, "In Defense of Earthquakes"

Trembling earth and exploding volcanoes are geology in action. This is geo-violence, and it exhilarates those who like great moments in geologic history. While shaking earth and erupting volcanoes hardly loom large among most people's images of Texas, the state has a real history of volcanic eruptions and earthquakes. Future geologic violence, too, is a real possibility.

Texas Volcanoes

Texas has abundant Precambrian and some Paleozoic igneous rocks as evidence of past volcanic activity, but time and erosion have long since removed all traces of the associated volcanoes. Erosion, however, has not completely destroyed our Mesozoic and Cenozoic volcanoes. Some extinct late Mesozoic volcanoes lie buried and preserved beneath younger sediment, and Cenozoic volcanoes of the Trans-Pecos region, although badly eroded, can still be recognized and mapped by geologists. In addition, volcanic activity in New Mexico is so recent and so tantalizingly close to the Texas border that it is tempting to speculate about future Texas volcanic eruptions.

Mesozoic Volcanoes

Many people are surprised to learn that volcanic rock is occasionally encountered in construction projects within Austin's city limits, and that Pilot Knob, a topographic landmark just outside the city, actually is an extinct Mesozoic volcano (Young, Caran, and Ewing 1981). The Uvalde area boasts an even higher concentration of extinct volcanoes. An excellent example is the Knippa "traprock" quarry near Uvalde (fig. 5.1), where beautifully columnar-jointed basalt is unceremoniously crushed to provide material for railway beds (Ewing, Caran, and Hudson 1986).

Since the mid-nineteenth century, geologists have recognized the

74

FIG. 5.1. Well-developed columnar joints in Mesozoic basalt at the
Knippa traprock quarry. Photo by author.

igneous nature of rocks interlayered with late Mesozoic (Cretaceous period) limestone along the Balcones Fault zone from Austin to Uvalde.
Some confusing terminology developed after the turn of the century,
when petroleum geologists started finding oil above and around subsurface green masses of rock over which limestone beds were draped. They
called the green rock mounds "serpentine plugs," an erroneous name
that persists in the literature today. Actually, the rocks contain very little
serpentine, and few can be shown to have intruded into the limestone,
as the word *plug* suggests. We now know that many of these "serpentine
plugs" actually are the eroded and altered remnants of extinct volcanoes.
Some of the volcanoes appear to have formed small volcanic islands,
bordered by reefs, in the shallow, tropical Cretaceous sea. As they formed,
the interaction of magma and sea water caused colossal steam explosions, forming low volcanic cones called *tuff rings* or even flatter volcanic
forms termed *maar volcanoes*. Alteration by sea water gave the volcanic
ash a greenish tint, and burial by calcareous sediment completed the formation of the "serpentine plugs" of the petroleum geology literature.

FIG. 5.2. The Mule Ears in Big Bend National Park were fashioned by erosion of rock away from two parallel-trending, shallow igneous intrusions.
Courtesy *Texas Highways.*

The Balcones igneous province follows the same general trend as the Balcones Fault zone (fig. 4.2), although a genetic relationship between volcanism and faulting has yet to be established. The igneous province is divided into two fields, the Travis volcanic field to the northeast and the Uvalde igneous field to the southwest (Ewing and Caran 1982). Volcanic activity appears to have reached its maximum about 84 million years ago, and more than two hundred occurrences of volcanic rock are presently known.

Cenozoic Volcanoes

The results of Cenozoic magmatism are found abundantly across Trans-Pecos Texas, from El Paso to Big Bend National Park. Geologists call this the Trans-Pecos volcanic field. Viewed on a continental scale, the Trans-Pecos field is but a small eroded bit left from a period of Cenozoic volcanism that affected most of western North America, and it is the most easterly expression of that volcanic episode. The ages of Trans-Pecos volcanic rocks are fairly well known, and a summary has been published (Henry and McDowell 1986).

The oldest igneous rock recognized thus far is prominently exposed on the campus of the University of Texas at El Paso. Although it is not a volcano, the Campus Andesite, as the rock appropriately is called, has an age of 48 million years. If you are a football fan, you've probably seen it. Each year during a lull in action on the field, one of the Sun Bowl's television cameras inevitably zooms in on one special group of spectators, a flock of football fans perched high atop a nearby hill with a free, albeit distant, view of the festivities below. That hill and much of the surrounding area is composed of Campus Andesite, which intruded into the surrounding sedimentary rocks during early Cenozoic time.

Trans-Pecos volcanism continued sporadically at widely scattered locations from 48 million to 39 million years ago and became extremely vigorous from 38 million to 32 million years ago, when great volumes of pyroclastic rocks spewed from major vents throughout Trans-Pecos Texas. Some volcanic rocks and shallow igneous intrusions are prominently displayed in Big Bend National Park (fig. 5.2). The Davis Mountains, located north of Alpine and home of McDonald Observatory, contain the largest contiguous exposures of Trans-Pecos volcanic rock (fig. 5.3). It has recently been determined that most of this thick sequence of Cenozoic volcanic rock erupted during a relatively short, violent interval of 1.4 million years, which took place between 38 million and 36 million years ago. Trans-Pecos volcanic activity began to wane 32 million years ago, and no volcanic rocks have yet yielded ages of from 27 million to 24 million years. Beginning at 24 million years and continuing until 17 million years ago, however, basaltic lava eruptions were widespread but minor in terms of volume of material ejected. This volcanism coincided with a major phase of faulting that broke much of Trans-Pecos Texas into a series of basins and ranges. Although faulting continues in Texas to the present day, the last known basalt eruption occurred 17 million years ago at Cox Mountain, northwest of Van Horn.

Possible Future Volcanic Eruptions

Texas certainly will have erupting volcanoes in the distant future, when plate motions change and either the Pacific or the Gulf of Mexico begins thrusting under North America. But what about the possibility of volcanic eruptions during our lifetime? There is a real, if slim,

FIG. 5.3. A road cut west of Alpine, Texas, exposes the side of an igneous dike trending parallel to U.S. Interstate Highway 10. Note how the flow direction of the magma is "frozen" in the igneous rock. Photo by author.

possibility that a Texas volcano might erupt in the next few thousand years, long before the plates change their motion. In fact, recently active basaltic volcanoes in eastern New Mexico are so close to Texas that we could almost claim them as part of our extraterritorial jurisdiction (fig. 5.4). Several of these volcanic fields have been active during the last million years; that's yesterday in terms of geologic time.

The Potrillo volcanic field (Wood and Kienle 1990), located just northwest of El Paso (fig. 5.4), is one of a number of basaltic volcanic fields related to the Rio Grande Rift. The area has more than 150 cinder cones and 1 small shield volcano (Aden Crater); it has at least 540 square miles of basaltic lava. In addition, there are 5 maar volcanoes, including Kilbourne Hole (fig. 5.5), a maar famous for having ejected numerous basalt-covered chunks plucked from the Earth's mantle far below. There have been no historic eruptions, but many of the field's volcanic features look extremely youthful. Aden Crater is believed to have formed about 16,000 years ago, and Kilbourne Hole may be only slightly older.

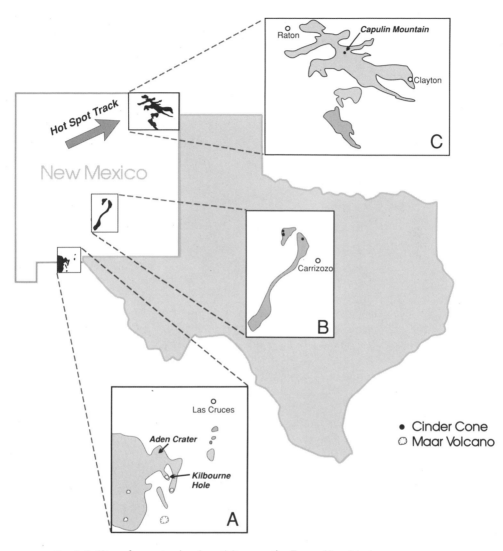

FIG. 5.4. Sites of recent volcanic activity near the Texas–New Mexico border. Map by Nancy Place; adapted from Wood and Kienle (1990).

FIG. 5.5. Kilbourne Hole, a maar volcano west of El Paso, Texas, formed when basaltic magma encountered abundant surface or near-surface water. The resulting steam explosions produced this enormous hole. Photo by author.

Geologically recent lava flows, lava tubes, and cinder cones also are found east of the Rio Grande, in a remote area of New Mexico near White Sands Missile Range (fig. 5.4) (Wood and Kienle 1990). The White Sands area includes the Carrizozo Basalt, a flow more than forty miles long that erupted from three cinder cones as recently as four thousand years ago. The volcanoes of the Potrillo volcanic field and those near White Sands are related to the Rio Grande Rift, a zone of crustal extension marked by the Rio Grande Valley, earthquakes, and recent volcanic activity. The western margin of the Rio Grande Rift extends southward into Texas, and volcanic activity along it, while unlikely in our lifetime, certainly is a possibility.

The Raton-Clayton volcanic field (Muehlberger et al. 1967) is located near New Mexico's borders with Colorado, Oklahoma, and Texas (fig. 5.4). The field occurs where the North American plate is believed to be moving westward over the "Raton hot spot," an area of mantle upwelling and melting that is now beneath northeastern New Mexico. A similar hot spot is thought to lie under northwestern Wyoming, where it has given rise to Yellowstone's recent volcanism, hot springs, and geysers.

The Raton-Clayton volcanic field has been active volcanically for the past 8 million years, but its youngest volcano is only about 2,300 years old. That volcano is Capulin Mountain, a scoria cone more than a thousand feet high and a designated national monument. An artifact known as the Folsom Point was found embedded in the skeleton of an extinct species of buffalo in sediment underlying basalt erupted from Capulin Mountain. This dramatically demonstrates that volcanism occurred after the arrival of humans to the area, although it is probably speculation that the Folsom Point was left by early Texans hunting big game in New Mexico.

Given the geologic history of the Raton area, it is entirely reasonable to expect the hot spot to fuel future volcanic eruptions. Meanwhile, North America continues its westward slide over the Raton hot spot, bringing Oklahoma and Texas ever closer to Raton's next volcanic eruption.

Texas Earthquakes

Earthquake hazard maps of the United States show Texas to be one of the least seismically active states in the Union, but earthquakes do occur here. Davis, Pennington, and Carlson (1989), of the Texas Bureau of Economic Geology, have reviewed Texas earthquake activity from 1847 to 1986. Their data show 106 quakes of magnitude 3 or greater (fig. 5.6). A magnitude 3 quake on the Richter scale generally can be felt in the epicenter area, and there are reports showing that 86 of the 106 events were felt. Texas averages about one quake per year of magnitude 3 or greater, but it must be remembered that earthquakes usually come in clusters of foreshocks and aftershocks closely spaced around the main event. Of the 106 Texas quakes, 24 were associated with some degree of damage, and one resident of Ciudad Juárez, Mexico, died when his adobe house collapsed during a 1923 quake (estimated magnitude of 4.7) in the Ciudad Juárez–El Paso area.

Table 5.1 lists the most significant historic Texas earthquakes. The largest known Texas earthquake occurred in 1931 near the West Texas town of Valentine. The main shock had an estimated magnitude of 6.0 and was part of a cluster of seismic events. The quake produced widespread damage and was felt for more than three hundred miles in all directions. Earthquake strength increases exponentially on the Richter scale. Thus, the great Alaska quake of 1964 had a Richter magnitude of

Table 5.1 Important Texas Earthquakes, 1847–1995

Date	Size	Location	Comments
14 Feb. 1847	3.5*	Seguin	Damaged houses at Seguin and New Braunfels
8 Jan. 1891	4.0*	Rusk	Several chimneys downed
7 Mar. 1923	4.7*	El Paso	Collapse of an adobe house kills a man in Juarez; windows broken in El Paso
30 Jul. 1925	5.4*	Panhandle	A cracked cistern, fallen chimney, cracked plaster, broken coal bin, and damaged railroad track reported
16 Aug. 1931	6.0*	Valentine	Two foreshocks and eight aftershocks reported 16–26 Aug. Moderate to severe damage to buildings; landslides near Valentine
20 Jun. 1936	5.0*	Borger	Dishes broken and buildings cracked at Pampa
12 Mar. 1948	5.2*	Dalhart	Cracks in plaster
20 Jun. 1951	4.2*	Amarillo	Cracks in plaster
19 Mar. 1957	4.7*	Gladewater	Followed by three aftershocks
28 Apr. 1964	4.4	Hemphill	Small ground fissure and cracked plaster. One of a cluster of eleven quakes 24 Apr.–3 June
14 Aug. 1966	3.4	Kermit	Windows broken
15 Feb. 1974	4.5	Perryton	Glass broken, walls cracked
16 Jun. 1978	4.6	Snyder	Windows broken
14 Oct. 1982	3.9	Dalhart	Crack in a parking lot
23 Jul. 1983	3.4	Fashing	Gasoline plant boiler shut down by shaking
3 Mar. 1984	3.9	Pleasanton	Plaster cracked and concrete cracks widened
9 Apr. 1993	4.2	Pleasanton, Jourdanton	On 16 May, a 3.0 quake followed
13 Apr. 1995	5.6	Alpine	Felt as far away as San Antonio

Source: Davis et al. (1989)

*Magnitudes of all pre-1964 quakes are estimates

8.5 and also was noticed in Texas. It generated large fluctuations in Texas water wells, caused water to slosh over the sides of swimming pools, and produced waves called *seiches* which damaged some boats in channels along the Gulf of Mexico.

The data on 106 earthquakes compiled by Davis, Pennington, and Carlson (1989) reveal a disturbing trend of increasing frequency in earthquake activity. Over half (59) of the quakes have occurred in the last twenty-three years. Better reporting of seismic events surely explains some of this apparent increase, but the trend of increasing seismicity is probably real. It appears that we are dealing with two types of quakes. While some are the result of the natural release of tectonic stresses along faults, others represent a premature release of stress induced by some oil and gas operations.

Natural Earthquakes

West Texas seismic activity, from El Paso to the Valentine area, appears to be related to faulting caused by extension of the crust along the Rio Grande Rift (fig. 5.6). Quakes in the Texas Panhandle have epicenters lying above a prominent structural feature believed to be the southern margin of an ancient rift (Southern Oklahoma Aulacogen) formed during the opening of the Iapetus Ocean in early Paleozoic time. A similar rift feature in the central United States may be responsible for increased seismicity there, including the three great 1811–12 shocks (of magnitudes estimated to range from 7.1 to 7.4) centered on New Madrid, Missouri. Old faults along these ancient rifts apparently become reactivated at infrequent intervals to relieve stresses that slowly develop in great crustal plates. Although the largest historic earthquake in the Texas Panhandle had a magnitude of only 5.4, this area, because of its similarity to the New Madrid area, is viewed with some alarm by Davis, Pennington, and Carlson (1989).

Some seismic activity has been reported in East Texas from the Balcones Fault zone eastward to the coast (fig. 5.6). Although the Balcones Fault zone is generally considered to be inactive, Davis, Pennington, and Carlson (1989) suggest that the earthquakes that occurred just east of Austin in 1873 and 1902 were caused by movement along the eastern part of the Balcones Fault system. Earthquakes along similar fault zones nearer the Gulf have been related to minor crustal adjustments in response to continued sediment deposition on the Gulf of Mexico side of the fault.

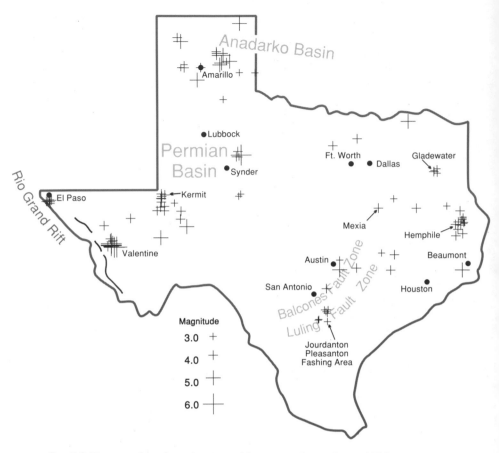

Fɪɢ. 5.6. Texas earthquake epicenters with measured or estimated Richter magnitudes of 3.0 or greater experienced between 1847 and 1986.
Map by Nancy Place; adapted from Davis et al. (1989).

A burst of earthquake activity occurred in 1964 in the Hemphill-Pineland area near the Sabine River, an area that currently lies between the Sam Rayburn and Toledo Bend reservoirs. Water impounded in reservoirs is known to induce earthquakes, but neither reservoir existed at the time of the quakes. The seismicity may be related to the subsidence of Gulf Coastal Plain sediment in response to continued loading of sediment derived from the continent's interior.

Induced Earthquakes

In addition to natural seismicity, earthquakes can be triggered by withdrawal of ground water and petroleum, or they may be induced by fluid injection to enhance the recovery of petroleum. Seismic events have been related to oil and gas operations near the Permian Basin towns of Kermit and Snyder, in East Texas near Mexia and Gladewater, and in South Texas at Fashing and Pleasanton (fig. 5.6). The Gladewater quake of 1957 probably was the largest of these quakes. It had an estimated magnitude of 4.7, the same as that estimated for the 1923 El Paso quake.

Volcanic eruptions in Texas are a future possibility, but my guess is that, when the next volcano bursts into life somewhere out there on the range, it will be in the Cascade Range.

Damaging earthquakes occasionally occur in Texas, but when America's next "big one" hits, it's more likely to target San Francisco than San Antonio.

References

Davis, S. D.; W. D. Pennington; and S. M. Carlson. 1989. *A compendium of earthquake activity in Texas.* Geological Circular 89–3. Austin: Bureau of Economic Geology, University of Texas at Austin. 27p.

Ewing, T., and S. Caran. 1982. Late Cretaceous volcanism in South and Central Texas: stratigraphic, structural, and seismic models. *Gulf Coast Association of Geological Societies Transactions* 32: 137–45.

Ewing, T.; S. Caran; and L. Hudson. 1986. *Late Cretaceous igneous rocks of the Uvalde area of Southwest Texas.* San Antonio: South Texas Geological Society. 37p.

Henry, C. D.; and F. W. McDowell. 1986. Geochronology of magmatism in the Tertiary volcanic field, Trans-Pecos Texas. In *Igneous geology of Trans-Pecos Texas,* edited by J. G. Price, C. D. Henry, D. F. Parker, and D. S. Barker, 99–122. Guidebook 23. Austin: Bureau of Economic Geology, University of Texas at Austin.

Muehlberger, W.; B. Baldwin; and R. Foster. 1967. *High Plains, northeastern New Mexico.* Scenic Trips to the Geologic Past, no. 7. Socorro, N.M.: New Mexico Bureau Mines and Mineral Resources. 107p.

Young, K.; B. Caran; and T. Ewing. 1981. *Cretaceous volcanism in the Austin area, Texas.* Guidebook 4. Austin, Tex.: Austin Geological Society. 68p.

Wood, Charles A., and J. Kienle. 1990. *Volcanoes of North America.* Cambridge: Cambridge University Press. 354p.

6 Texas Minerals and Fossils

Lives of great men all remind us
We can make our lives sublime,
And, departing, leave behind us
Footprints on the sands of time.
—Longfellow, "Psalm of Life"

People naturally are attracted to the brilliant colors and intricate patterns of agate, the cool geometric precision of gems and crystals, and the mysterious stony remains of life forms long extinct. Texas has rocks, minerals, and fossils in abundance, as well as legions of devoted rock hounds who leave no stone unturned in their pursuit of these million-year-old natural works of art. Not all rock hounds, however, are alike. While some are eagerly sniffing out, digging up, and lapping pretty rocks into bookends, belt buckles, and bolo ties, others doggedly track down rare minerals or fossil bones. Appendix A contains addresses of rock clubs devoted to a variety of interests.

Texas Minerals and Gems

F. W. Simonds in 1902 published the first and, for a long time, the only attempt at a comprehensive description of Texas minerals. In the 1960s, the Bureau of Economic Geology of the University of Texas at Austin issued two useful and informative pamphlets. *Texas Gemstones* (King 1961) covers a few gems and a large variety of minerals and rocks suitable for cutting and polishing. *Texas Rocks and Minerals: An Amateur's Guide* (Girard 1964) describes rock types and the physical properties of minerals, and offers a long list of common Texas rocks and minerals.

Other sources include a modest effort, *Rock Hunting in Texas* (Gronberg and Nutting 1986), and a fairly good account of fifty-six Texas rock, mineral, and fossil collecting sites, *Gem Trails of Texas* (Mitchell 1987). The most comprehensive description of Texas minerals to date, however, is the "Texas Mineral Locality Index" (Smith 1991). An essential resource for the serious mineral collector, the index appeared in *Rocks and Minerals*, a magazine well known to mineral and fossil fans.

A comprehensive review of Texas minerals is beyond the scope of this book, but mention must be made here of several Texas gems and of Baringer Hill and Terlingua, crown jewels among Texas mineral localities.

In the early part of this century, Baringer Hill stood on the west bank of the Colorado River between Llano and Burnet. The site became the source of some of this country's most highly prized rare-earth-element minerals. Baringer Hill pegmatite (pegmatite is an igneous rock with an extremely large average grain size) contains these rare minerals. In addition to their uncommon chemical composition, many Baringer Hill specimens are radioactive, and it is radiation damage that accounts for the smoky color of some Baringer Hill quartz crystals. Some of these crystals weighed over one thousand pounds each. But if you think a stop at Baringer Hill might fit nicely into your vacation plans, be advised that this wonderful mineral locality has been underwater since 1938, when Buchanan Dam was completed across the Colorado River.

A second classic Texas mineral location is the Terlingua mining district near Big Bend National Park. Terlingua was a mercury mining area and the discovery site for many rare mercury minerals. The most famous mineral collecting location is the now-defunct Mariposa mine. Terlinguaite, a tongue-twister of a mineral named for the region's major town, is among the many mercury minerals first identified here.

By far the most treasured Texas gem is high-quality topaz from Mason County in the Central Mineral Region. Around the turn of the century, folks started finding topaz in Mason County's recent stream gravel and ancient granite. Topaz containing gem pockets formed in the region's coarse-grained granite about 1 billion years ago. The stones are extremely difficult to locate, and likely source areas are located almost exclusively on private land. Frosted pebbles, however, still can be found in the area's stream gravel, and these ordinary-looking stones are still being cut into brilliant gemstones. Pure topaz is colorless, and Texas topaz is usually colorless or white. Some Mason County topaz, however, has a strikingly beautiful, pale blue color that makes it among the world's best. One exquisite, pale-blue crystal weighed in at 1,296 grams (2.85 pounds) and now resides in the Smithsonian Museum in Washington, D.C. Topaz looks a lot like common quartz, but it is harder and heavier. It also splits or cleaves to form a flat surface, while quartz breaks along a curved fracture. Blue topaz has been designated as the official state gem, and there is now even an official Lone Star cut developed in the shape of a Texas star (fig. 6.1).

Fɪɢ. 6.1. Mason County topaz displaying the Lone Star cut. Courtesy *Texas Highways*.

Among the remaining long list of Texas rocks and gems, two generate special interest. The first is amber, a fossil resin found in coal beds near Eagle Pass. The second is one small diamond found in 1911, lying in loose sand and gravel west of Wichita Falls (Sterrett 1912). The diamond, described as rough, brownish, and fairly clear, was workable into a quarter-carat stone. Thousands of diamonds have been recovered from Crater of Diamonds State Park near Murfreesboro, Arkansas. Diamonds were discovered there in 1906, and the Arkansas diamonds' source diamond pipes—cylindrically shaped igneous rock through which the diamonds are forced from deep within the earth to near the earth's surface—are well known. The source for that one Texas diamond, however, is unknown, and the diamond remains an enigma.

Fossils

Fossils are the remains or traces of life from the geologic past, and they are really rather special. Only rarely is the passage of a life preserved in stone. Very few animal or plant remains survive long enough after the organism's death to be preserved. It usually requires quick burial followed by mineralization of pore space or chemical replacement of the organism. Traces of an organism's existence preserved in stone are also considered fossils. Trace fossils include such things as casts, molds,

Fig. 6.2. A dinosaur fight staged by the Fort Worth Museum of Science and History. Courtesy *Texas Highways*.

tracks, and trails. The UT Bureau of Economic Geology's *Texas Fossils: An Amateur Collector's Handbook* (Matthews 1960) offers many illustrations to help amateur paleontologists identify their discoveries. Finsley's *A Field Guide to Texas Fossils* (1989), more recent and more comprehensive, contains a large number of excellent photographs of fossil specimens. Texas dinosaurs are covered in several attractive formats. *Pathway to the Dinosaurs* (Jenkins and Jenkins 1989) is a very informative map with explanatory text, while *Dinosaur Days in Texas* (Tom Allen and Jane Allen with Savannah Waring Walker 1989) is a more comprehensive book. *Cretaceous Airport* (Jacobs 1993) is a booklet telling the surprising story of dinosaurs and other Mesozoic monsters that swaggered and swam through the area now occupied by Dallas–Fort Worth International Airport. Louis Jacobs' *Texas Dinosaurs* (1995), published by Texas A&M University Press, offers a beautifully illustrated and comprehensive examination of the dinosaur era in the Lone Star State. Fossils may also be examined at close range in several natural history museums around the state (fig. 6.2 and see appendix F).

Fossil remains and traces are almost exclusively found in sediments deposited during the past 570 million years. These are the Phanerozoic (from Greek root words meaning visible life) sedimentary rocks, and rocks of every Phanerozoic era and period are found in Texas (see fig. 4.1 for the geologic time scale). When all Texas fossils, microscopic to dinosaurs, are considered, it is estimated that Texas rocks may contain well over half a million fossil species (Finsley 1989).

Paleozoic Rocks and Fossils

In the early part of the Paleozoic (from Greek root words for ancient life) era, life was developing in the oceans. Cambrian rocks—those from the era's oldest period—are exposed in the Central Mineral Region, the Franklin Mountains near El Paso, and in the Marathon area of West Texas. Although there was an explosion of invertebrate life, in terms of abundance and diversity, at the beginning of the Cambrian period, and brachiopods and trilobites are locally abundant, complete Cambrian fossils are not plentiful in Texas.

Ordovician rocks are more widespread and Ordovician fossils more abundant. Fossil sponges, corals, brachiopods, gastropods, cephalopods, and trilobites are contained in rocks at the three previously mentioned locations. Additionally, well-preserved graptolites are found in Ordovician rocks of the Marathon area.

Silurian rocks are poorly represented in Texas, but Silurian brachiopods and corals are found in abundance in the Franklin Mountains at El Paso.

All three locations have Devonian rocks containing corals, brachiopods, gastropods, and trilobites. Primitive armored fish swim into the picture during Devonian time, and fish fragments also are found.

Mississippian period rocks are found around the Central Mineral Region, near Marathon, and in the Hueco Mountains east of El Paso. They contain brachiopods, gastropods, cephalopods, trilobites, bryozoans, crinoids, and ostracodes.

Rocks of the Pennsylvanian period are abundantly exposed in the Marathon area and in a wide band across North-Central Texas. The Pennsylvanian period was a great coal-forming time, and coal beds and plant fossils are found locally, as are marine corals, brachiopods, bryozoans, gastropods, pelecypods, and foraminifera (fig. 6.3). Fusulinids, one-celled, shelled organisms resembling stony grains of wheat, can be added to this list. They characterize Pennsylvanian rocks, as well as those of the Permian period, the last of the Paleozoic era.

FIG. 6.3. Some typical late Paleozoic (Pennsylvanian) marine fossils in limestone. Courtesy *Texas Highways*.

The Permian period is named after a former Russian province, but experts consider the Texas Permian section second to none. Texas Permian rocks include some of the fiery-colored rocks exposed along the eastern caprock escarpment at Palo Duro Canyon and Caprock Canyons state parks. They also include the magnificent barrier reef so prominently displayed in the Guadalupe Mountains. In the subsurface, an enormous thickness of Permian shale, salt, gypsum, and oil-rich limestone form what quite appropriately is called the Permian Basin. A very special exposure of Permian rocks crops out in the Glass Mountains of Brewster County. Fossils there have been silicified, making it possible for acid to free wonderfully preserved specimens from their enclosing limestone. Silica has even replaced the soft tissue of some of these fossils, allowing a rare glimpse at the internal organs of shellfish that have been off the menu for 250 million years. The Permian period ended the Paleozoic era. It was a time of extinction for many invertebrate groups, but also a time in which the vertebrates that were precursors to the Mesozoic dinosaurs flourished.

Mesozoic Rocks and Fossils

Mesozoic (Greek for middle life) sedimentary rocks, while abundant and widespread in Texas, have a peculiar character. Cretaceous rock covers an impressive 28 percent of the state, but older Triassic and Jurassic rocks have very little surface expression at all. The explanation is simple. Rocks of the Mesozoic and Cenozoic eras are related to the Gulfian sedimentary cycle, which continues today with sedimentation at the coast. Because younger sediments are deposited on older rocks, Triassic and Jurassic rocks are mostly concealed beneath younger Cretaceous and Cenozoic sedimentary rocks. Cretaceous rocks, however, form a major exception to this pattern, because they were deposited when the sea extended far out from the Gulf to cover Texas and indeed much of the western United States. Since Cretaceous days, uplift in the west has shifted sedimentation back to the continent's edge, leaving Cretaceous rocks high and dry in many parts of central and western Texas.

Erosion has exposed Triassic rocks in parts of North and West Texas and, most noticeably, along the Canadian River, at Caprock Canyons and Palo Duro Canyon state parks, where colorful Triassic sandstone and shale overlie similar-looking Permian rocks. Most of these rocks were deposited in sedimentary basins above sea level. As such, their fossils include plant remains and fossil vertebrates such as crocodiles, turtles, and fish.

Jurassic exposures are even more limited in Texas. A little Jurassic sandstone, limestone, and shale are found in far West Texas, where they contain marine invertebrate fossils, including ammonites.

The Cretaceous rocks form a wide belt of bedded limestone exposed prominently from Santa Elena Canyon in Big Bend National Park to the Central Texas Hill Country, and less conspicuously into Northeast Texas. Cretaceous invertebrate fossils are abundant. Among the most common forms are pelecypods, cephalopods, gastropods, and echinoids (fig. 6.4). In addition, the Glen Rose Formation is famous for trails left by dinosaurs crossing the limy mud flats of what in Cretaceous time was the Texas coastal plain.

Dinosaurs! That's what paleontology is all about for most people. Forget spineless sponges and brainless bryozoans; bring on those legendary lizards! Although actual remains are rather rare, an ever-growing number of Texas dinosaur trackways attest to their having been here in significant numbers. Texas had at least sixteen of the approximately three hundred different kinds of dinosaurs known worldwide.

Fig. 6.4. Some typical Cretaceous marine fossils.
Courtesy *Texas Highways.*

The oldest dinosaurs are found in fossil-bearing Triassic formations exposed along the breakes and escarpments of the Southern High Plains. One of the oldest sounds more like a late model just off the evolutionary assemble line: *Technosaurus,* named for Texas Tech University at Lubbock, near where teeth and bones of this animal were discovered. *Technosaurus* ate plants, had two feet, and was slightly built and about four feet long. *Coelophysis* was another early two-legged, lightly-built, Panhandle dinosaur. *Coelophysis,* however, was a speedy meat-eater.

Before we leave the Texas High Plains and Triassic times, there is one other fossil currently raising a big flap. It's a birdlike creature dubbed *Protoavis* (first bird). *Protoavis* bones are dinosaur-like, but skull fragments show large, birdlike eye sockets, the hollow wing and leg bones needed to reduce weight for flight, and what could be described as the world's oldest "wish bone," a fused collarbone structure needed to support flapping wings. The crow-size "bird" predates the well-known reptile-bird transition fossil, *Archaeopteryx,* by 75 million years, but was it really a bird? The Texas discovery has generated significant debate.

Protoavis was discovered in Triassic sediments of the Dockum Formation near Post, thirty miles southeast of Lubbock. *Technosaurus* and many other fossils have come from this remarkable quarry dubbed "Triassic Park" by local geologists.

Only a few Jurassic rocks are exposed in Texas, and no Jurassic dinosaurs have yet been described. Cretaceous rocks, on the other hand, are widespread in Texas, and these have produced most of the Texas dinosaurs, as well as an abundance of dinosaur tracks and trails.

Acrocanthosaurus and *Pleurocoelus* are two Cretaceous Texans forever linked in a gripping drama played out near Fort Worth. *Acrocanthosaurus* was a large Tyrannosaurus-like meat-eater, while *Pleurocoelus* was an even larger vegetarian that probably roamed the range in a herd. *Acrocanthosaurus* may have weighed two or three tons and was, perhaps, thirty feet from nose to tailtip. Both dinosaurs are known from remains in West-Central Texas and south of Fort Worth.

In the latter location, one of the world's most famous dinosaur pathways is exposed along the bed of the Paluxy River. George Adams, a truant schoolboy, took note of them in 1908 and reported them to his teacher (Farlow 1993). They were recognized as dinosaur footprints in 1917, and ultimately two basic types were described. The most abundant tracks were made by dinosaurs walking on two birdlike feet, each foot having three toes (fig. 6.5). The other, larger prints, however, belonged to a four-legged creature with round rear-foot tracks more than a yard wide. The larger tracks are believed to have been made by the monstrous herbivore *Pleurocoelus*. The prints resemble potholes, except for the raised rim formed when the now-solidified mud was pushed up around the feet of this ponderous beast. Also, these "potholes" occur in distinctive trails of evenly spaced steps that alternate in size as if produced by front and back feet of different dimensions.

One *Pleurocoelus* trail appears to be followed by another trail, made by a three-toed, two-legged creature, possibly the meat-eating *Acrocanthosaurus*. It is easy to imagine a titanic melodrama being played out on the Glen Rose mudflats, as a ferocious killer stalks a prey ten times its own enormous weight.

In Cretaceous days, when the tracks were made, the place where the Paluxy River now runs was a low-lying coastal area with offshore reefs and lagoons, similar in many ways to South Florida. Dinosaurs strolled across the limy tidal flats and waded in the shallow lagoons. Some tracks made in the sticky lime dried brick-hard in the sun, and a few of these were buried before they could be destroyed, probably by sediment

FIG. 6.5. Foot track of a large Theropod dinosaur at Dinosaur Valley State Park. Courtesy *Texas Highways.*

carried in when nearby rivers ran high. As the Cretaceous seas advanced over the land, the tracks remained locked beneath layers of rock, await-ing uplift and retreat of the sea. The tracks, buried and preserved be-neath a layer of softer sediment for millions of years, now are exposed, due to erosion by the Paluxy River. These and other dinosaur tracks are on public display sixty miles southwest of Fort Worth at Dinosaur Valley State Park.

Other dinosaur trails have been found in Bandera, Blanco, Comal, Kimble, Medina, Montague, Somervell, and Wise counties (fig. 6.6). Trails of twenty-three sauropods at the Bandera County location suggest that the animals were traveling as a herd, with the smaller-footed young ones in a protected central position. New tracks, like those found in Austin's Zilker Park in the winter of 1992, are always being discovered.

Ornithomimus is an ostrichlike dinosaur known from Cretaceous rocks of the Big Bend area. It had no teeth but may have snatched eggs or

FIG. 6.6. A large Sauropod track in the bed of the Blanco River.
Photo by author.

eaten insects, small reptiles, and vegetation. Other known Texas vegetarian dinosaurs, from smallest to largest, are the bony-headed *Stegoceras*, *Tenontosaurus, Chasmosaurus, Panoplosaurus, Hadrosaurus, Edmontosaurus, Iguanodon, Torosaurus, Alamosaurus,* and the previously mentioned *Pleurocoelus.* Cretaceous carnivores from Texas, from smallest to largest, are *Deinonychus,* the aforementioned *Acrocanthosaurus,* and *Tyrannosaurus.*

Tyrannosaurus Rex, of course, is the most famous of the dinosaurs. Skull fragments and a tooth of this late Cretaceous monster have been found in rocks of the Big Bend region. *Tyrannosaurus* may have weighed six tons and had jaws three feet deep that were fringed by seven-inch, razor-edged teeth. While only incomplete fragments have been found in Texas, it should be noted that complete skulls of *Tyrannosaurus* are extremely rare, and any nearly complete dinosaur skeleton is a find of major proportions.

What are a group's chances of traveling to West Texas and finding a fossil dinosaur? Remote. Yet that is just what a student group from the University of Chicago did during its spring break in 1991. Tom Evans, a senior biology major, found the five-foot-long skull and shield of a horned dinosaur, probably *Chasmosaurus,* previously known in Texas only from fragments. A relative of the better-known *Triceratops, Chasmosaurus* was a four-footed, 2.5-ton vegetarian with scary-looking armor and horns.

Soaring reptile relatives of the dinosaurs, *pterosaurs,* also have been found in Texas. These include the toothless *Pteranodon,* the toothy *Rhamphorhynchus,* and *Quetzalcoatlus,* another student discovery in Big Bend. *Quetzalcoatlus* (ket-sal-ko-át-lus) caused a sensation in the press when its discovery was announced. The reason lay in the size of its wing-span,

FIG. 6.7. Petrified palm wood from the Smithville–La Grange area, showing the typical dot pattern of palm wood known as "soda straws."
Courtesy *Texas Highways*.

estimated at forty-five feet—longer than the wings of some airplanes. *Quetzalcoatlus* is the largest flying creature ever found. *Quetzalcoatlus* takes its name from Quetzalcoatl, god of the Toltecs and Aztecs and represented as a plumed serpent. When *Quetzalcoatlus* soared, it must have looked like a glider. The animal may have lived along some late Cretaceous river, where it scavenged food like the modern vulture.

Phobosuchus was another gigantic Texas discovery. The fossil consisted of a massive skull some six feet long, belonging to a monster crocodile estimated to have been forty to fifty feet in length.

Other giant reptiles also lived during the time of the dinosaurs, and the remains of some of them have been found in Texas. *Mosasaurs,* large carnivorous reptiles with flippers like paddles and tooth-studded jaws, once prowled the Cretaceous seas and several now lurk in Texas museums (see Appendix F). Described as the last thing many fish ever saw, these beasts, fifteen to thirty feet long, were the "killer whales" of their age. Other Mesozoic marine reptiles, include the long-necked *Plesiosaurs* and perhaps the largest turtle of its type ever found, a twelve-foot *Protostega* discovered near Waco in 1971.

Cenozoic Rocks and Fossils

Cenozoic sedimentary rocks cover about one-third of the state, and they represent a diverse assemblage. The Texas Gulf Coastal Plain is the surface portion of a sedimentary wedge thickening toward the Gulf and reaching a thickness of up to fifty thousand feet! Obviously, only the driller's bit has seen more than the surface, but these rocks contain one fossil of great interest. The fossil that "hounds" probably seek more than any other is fossilized wood, especially palm wood, the official state stone of Texas (fig. 6.7). Palm wood is easily distinguished from other fossil wood because, instead of growth rings, a cross-section shows small, dotlike tubes that run through the middle of the wood. Fossil finds include limbs, large trunk fragments, and even stumps of silicified, agatized, and opalized wood.

Cenozoic sediment also forms a veneer over parts of Trans-Pecos Texas and much of the High Plains. Much of this sediment was transported by streams flowing from the Rocky Mountains. Animals lived and died along the banks of these streams; the Panhandle-Plains Historical Museum in Canyon has a nice display of Ice Age mammals that once roamed this region. These include skeletons of llamas, peccaries, dire wolves, mastodons, ground sloths, and saber-toothed cats.

The wet Ice Age (Pleistocene Epoch, 2 million to 10,000 years ago) climate intensively dissected parts of the High Plains, carving Palo Duro Canyon. It also enlarged river valleys such as that of the Pecos River to a size far greater than that required by the present-day streams. Much of this sediment found its way to the Texas Gulf Coast, where it forms some of the state's youngest deposits, but some was stranded on terraces fringing rivers. These river terrace sands and gravels occasionally yield the bony and toothy remains of horses, camels, mammoths, long-tusked mastodons, saber-toothed cats, and giant dire wolves.

Geologists often use fossils to tell the age of sedimentary rocks. Trilobites, for example, are guide fossils for the Paleozoic era, and dinosaurs belong to the Mesozoic. What do you suppose will be the index fossils for the Anthropozoic epoch (interval of human life)? Someday an alien field geologist might submit the following report:

> This epoch's dominant life form (neglecting fire ants) seems to have been a large featherless biped that developed the capacity to use energy derived from even older fossil species (fossil fuels). Like the giant sauropods at the end of the Mesozoic, this creature's energy requirements were great; it lived at a time characterized by pronounced changes to the land surface, rapidly shifting environmental conditions, profound ecosystem stress, and escalating extinction rates.
>
> Unlike the sauropods, this creature appears to have had some measure of control over its environment but failed to use this control in an adaptive manner. That conclusion is drawn from a

distinctive lithology, here termed civilizationite. Civilizationite consists of unprecedented levels of waste products, and it is the characteristic rock deposited during the last stages of the Anthropozoic epoch. It is analogous to the older K-T boundary layer, in that it marks the end of a geologic age, and no fossils of this extraordinary creature have been found above the civilizationite stratigraphic level.

"Leave only footprints," cautions the park ranger. Those creatures who strolled where the Paluxy River now runs did just that.

References

Allen, T.; J. Allen; and S. Walker. 1989. *Dinosaur days in Texas.* Dallas: Hendrick-Long Publishing Co. 64p.

Farlow, James O. 1993. *The dinosaurs of Dinosaur Valley State Park.* Austin: Texas Parks and Wildlife Press. 32p.

Finsley, Charles. 1989. *A field guide to fossils of Texas.* Austin: Texas Monthly Press. 188p. Address: Austin TX 78767.

Girard, R. M. 1964. *Texas rocks and minerals: an amateur's guide.* Guidebook 6. Austin: Bureau of Economic Geology, University of Texas at Austin. 109p.

Gronberg, M., and L. Nutting. 1986. *Rock hunting in Texas.* Houston: Lone Star Books. 90p.

Jacobs, L. 1993. *Cretaceous airport: the surprising story of real dinosaurs at DFW.* Dallas: Institute for the Study of Earth and Man. 25p. Address: Dallas TX 75275.

———. 1995. *Texas dinosaurs.* College Station: Texas A&M University Press. 176p.

Jenkins, John, and Jan Jenkins. 1989. *Pathway to the dinosaurs map no. 3: Texas.* 1 sheet. Englewood, Colo.: Dino Productions.

King, E. A., Jr. *Texas gemstones.* 1961. Report of Investigations No. 42. Austin: Bureau of Economic Geology, University of Texas at Austin. 42p.

Matthews, W. H., III. 1960. *Texas fossils: an amateur collector's handbook.* Guidebook 2. Austin: Bureau of Economic Geology, University of Texas at Austin. 123p.

Mitchell, James R. 1987. *Gem trails of Texas.* Pico Rivera, Calif.: Gem Guides Book Co. 104p. Address: Pico Rivera CA 90660.

Simonds, F. W. 1902. The minerals and mineral localities of Texas. *University of Texas Mineral Science Bulletin* 5.

Smith, A. E. 1991. Texas mineral locality index. *Rocks and Minerals* 66 (no. 3): 196–224.

Sterrett, D. 1912. Gems and precious stones. In *Mineral resources of the United States.* Part II: *Nonmetals,* 1023–1060. Washington, D.C: United States Geological Survey.

7 Texas Natural Resources

I'm Dad Joiner and I've just come from the Texas coast
with a dream you ought to know about.
—Columbus "Dad" Joiner, 1926

What Dad Joiner dreamed about was "Texas tea" (a crude term for petroleum) and where to find it. The *Texas Almanac* reports only twenty-two Texas counties with absolutely no oil production (although a number of Texas counties have no significant oil production). Fifteen Texas counties have produced over a billion barrels of oil each (table 7.1), and there are no fewer than fifty-four oil fields in which the ultimate recovery is expected to reach 100 million barrels of oil or more (fig. 7.1). Three of the world's fourteen largest oil provinces are located entirely or partly in Texas, and the state has produced about 55 billion barrels of petroleum—nearly 40 percent of the nation's historic production. Although Texas leads the states in petroleum production, there is more to natural resources than petroleum and natural gas.

Nonfuel resources are commonly classified as either metals or industrial rocks and minerals. Industrial rocks and minerals typically are those used by industry in large amounts (e.g., crushed rock and cement for roads and skyscrapers), although some are employed in small amounts for personal purposes (e.g., talc for baby's bottom). Texas, with an annual nonfuel mineral production valued at $1.5 billion, ranks sixth among the fifty states.

Keeping track of resources is one of the major functions of the Texas Bureau of Economic Geology. The bureau is what most states call a geological survey. Texas tried having a state survey, but it didn't work. From 1858 to 1905, four surveys were organized and then quickly left unfunded. Peter T. Flawn, a past director of the bureau, once observed, "Any organization carrying the name *survey* is short-lived in Texas."

By 1909, the geologists had figured out the problem and proposed a label with a more permanent ring: bureau. The Bureau of Economic Geology was established as a research entity at the University of Texas at

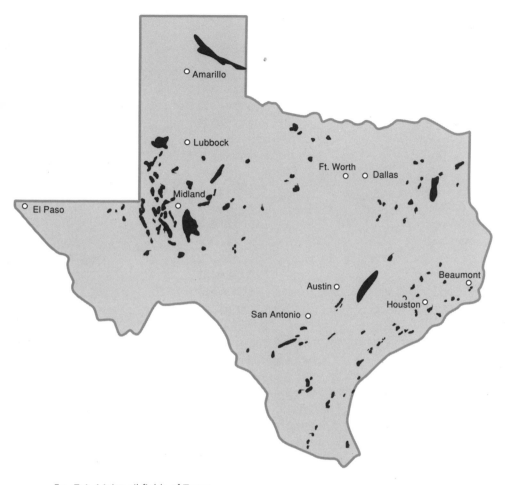

FIG. 7.1. Major oil fields of Texas.

Map by Nancy Place; adapted from Galloway et al. (1983).

Austin, where it functions as a state geologic survey supported by both public and private funds. Among many other duties, the bureau maintains computer files on active and inactive Texas mineral producers. It also has published a directory of nonpetroleum mineral producers (McBride and Dobbs 1983), an atlas of Texas oil reservoirs (Galloway et al. 1983), and maps showing Texas mineral resources (Garner et al. 1979). The bureau periodically issues topical reports: for example, Evans' *Gold*

Table 7.1   "Billion-Barrel" Petroleum Producing Counties of Texas

County	Total Production to 1 Jan. 1992
Gregg	3,135,670,672
Ector	2,795,773,124
Andrews	2,441,912,227
Scurry	1,849,444,265
Rusk	1,779,434,826
Gaines	1,755,036,573
Yoakum	1,728,125,073
Crane	1,586,864,665
Pecos	1,552,081,644
Harris	1,339,761,102
Hockley	1,334,515,296
Refugio	1,260,488,129
Brazoria	1,234,376,681
Wood	1,118,441,549
Winkler	1,018,305,126

Source: *Texas Almanac,* 1994–95

and Silver in Texas (1975). Texas oil and mineral production also is regularly treated in the *Texas Almanac.* This chapter gives a taste of Texas mineral resources, starting with a sip of "Texas Tea."

Fossil Fuels and Related Resources
Petroleum and Natural Gas

The first Europeans who arrived in Texas discovered, as had the Native Americans before them, that petroleum, in places, literally oozed from the Texas turf. Neither group, however, was greatly excited by the find. The Indians, like the "snake-oil" salesmen of later years, used petroleum for medicinal purposes, and Hernando de Soto's men used an oil seep's tarry residue to caulk their leaky ships. With no real demand for crude oil, it remained little more than a curiosity.

By the mid-eighteenth century, oil was being used in lubricants and lamps, but that oil was being unwillingly supplied by our blubbery marine friends, the whales. American whaling, in fact, was booming when

Drake's first oil well helped these creatures avoid extinction. Drake's well was drilled (pounded, actually) in Pennsylvania in 1859. New petroleum technology and the rediscovery of an ancient Arab method of distilling kerosene from petroleum spawned the petroleum industry and took some pressure off the whales.

Just seven years later, in 1866, a Nacogdoches County resident, Lyne T. Barret, used a rotary device to drill the first Texas oil well, all of 106 feet deep. Several other wells followed, but not much oil was produced. The first significant discovery, however small by later standards, came in June, 1894, when a water well being drilled for the town of Corsicana struck oil. Dismayed drillers cursed their luck, but a number of oil wells later were completed and a refinery built. The Texas petroleum industry was off to a modest start.

Beaumont means "beautiful mountain," but the name hardly described the small turn-of-the-century lumber town. Certainly the unusual rise located nearby was neither beautiful nor mountainous. The locals called it "Spindletop" for the way the summer heat caused shimmering waves to dance along the crest of the low mound, giving it the appearance of a spinning top. For a number of years, Pattillo Higgins had been convinced that oil lay beneath Spindletop, but he could find no financial backers for exploratory drilling.

It didn't help that eminent geologists scoffed at the idea. *Petroleum* means "rock oil," and petroleum is found in rock. Beaumont's water wells already had established that a great thickness of unconsolidated sediment underlay the city. What no one at the time realized was that great pillars of salt had risen in places along the Gulf Coast, dragging rock near the surface and creating petroleum traps (fig. 7.2). Spindletop, in fact, was the surface expression of a salt dome.

It was Anthony Lucas, an Austrian immigrant, who proved Higgins right. At 10:30 A.M. on January 10, 1901, after reaching a depth of 1,020 feet, the well Lucas drilled blew out, and during the next nine days it lubricated Spindletop with an estimated one million barrels of crude oil. A gusher was something new to the oil business, but finally the well was capped and buried. Other wells were drilled, and, within a short time (fig. 7.3), Spindletop was producing 94 percent of all the oil in Texas— more than the combined total from all other wells in the world!

Actually, the world didn't need that much oil in 1901, and the price dropped to an all-time low of three cents a barrel. Still, this was the world's first giant oil field and the first salt dome oil discovery. Spindletop helped

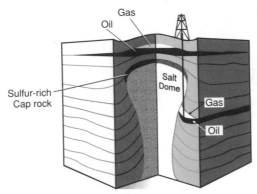

FIG. 7.2. Sketch of a typical Gulf Coast salt dome, with associated petroleum traps and caprock sulfur.
Drawing by Nancy Place.

to fuel the United States' shift to a petroleum-based economy, and Texas oil made the automobile possible. Although there had been earlier oil strikes, Spindletop marked the real beginning of the industry that would drive the state's economy for most of this century. J. A. Clark authored a delightful book (Clark 1952) chronicling the discovery of Spindletop.

The decade 1910–20 brought discoveries in the North-Central Plains in Eastland County east of Abilene, and in Wichita County around Wichita Falls. The 1920s brought a rash of discoveries, including oil in the Texas Panhandle, the Luling Field in South Texas, and the Mexia and second Powell fields in Limestone and Navarro counties south of Dallas. Of enormous significance to the economic and educational future of Texas, however, was the discovery of the Permian Basin.

Santa Rita is the patron saint of the impossible, and it was only after overcoming nearly impossible odds that the Santa Rita No. 1 well blew in on May 28, 1923. This well signaled the discovery of what would be many Permian Basin oil fields. The discovery, near Big Lake in Reagan County, happened to be on Permanent University Fund land, and it marked a turning point for higher education in Texas.

The Texas Constitution had set aside more than two million acres of land in West Texas for support of higher education. The funds derived from cattle leases, however, had been inadequate for the purpose. When Santa Rita came in, that changed. As of May 31, 1991, the Permanent University Fund had a book value of more than $3.2 billion. Many of the state's public college buildings stand as monuments to petroleum revenue. Even larger sums have gone to the Texas Permanent School Fund for public schools.

FIG. 7.3. Gladys City, the reconstructed Spindletop boom town at Beaumont. Photo by author.

Santa Rita No. 1 was brought to University of Texas at Austin campus in 1940. Although the original burned, a replica has been constructed at a remote corner of the campus, where a recorded message continuously tells the story mostly to birds, squirrels, and occasional passersby (fig. 7.4).

By 1928, Texas was leading the United States in crude oil production, a distinction never relinquished, but the biggest single field was yet to be discovered (Clark and Halbouty 1972). Texas legend has it that a seventy-year-old wildcatter, Columbus M. "Dad" Joiner, fell asleep on the Galveston seawall one day and dreamt that the biggest oil field in the world lay under Rusk County in East Texas. He claimed to have found the spot of his dreams on Daisy Bradford's farm near Henderson. Separately, "Doc" Lloyd, a three-hundred-pound, seventy-year-old former physician turned "geologist," had drawn straight lines on an oil field map of the U.S. and concluded that they intersected in East Texas.

In 1930, flaunting scientific geology, Lloyd and Joiner convinced a reluctant Daisy Bradford to let them drill on her farm. This strange pair

F_IG. 7.4. The Santa Rita No. 2, displayed at the Midland Petroleum Museum, dates from 1923. It was moved there from Texon, eighty miles to the southeast. Photo by author.

proceeded to drill two dry holes, but the third, the Daisy Bradford No. 3, erupted in a gusher. The East Texas field proved enormous. It stretched to Kilgore, then to Longview and beyond. Once again the flood of new petroleum overwhelmed the demand, and in 1930 the price dropped from $1.10 to 15 cents a barrel. Later, in the war against Japan, East Texas oil help the Allies "float to victory on a sea of oil," as Winston Churchill put it.

Oil in the East Texas field flows from the late Cretaceous Woodbine Formation. A petroleum trap was created when the formation was tilted on the flank of the Sabine Uplift so that Woodbine sandstone was exposed to erosion. The tilted, eroded edge later was buried by impermeable sediment, producing a type of stratigraphic trap known as an unconformity, or *pinch out,* in oil jargon.

The East Texas Oil Field has produced more than 5.1 billion barrels of oil, and its wells are still flowing. The field has made Gregg and Rusk counties numbers one and five, respectively, among the oil-producing counties of Texas (table 7.1). The East Texas field is the largest discovered in the continental U.S. (Prudhoe Bay in Alaska is about twice as big), but today the daily production from Gregg and Rusk counties is equaled or surpassed by at least five West Texas counties.

In fact, most of the significant, post-1930 oil discoveries were made in the Permian Basin. In consequence, West Texas has nine of the fifteen counties on the "billion barrel" list (table 7.1). The remaining four entries consist of Harris and Brazoria counties in the Houston area, Refugio County along the South Texas Gulf Coast, and Wood County, east of Dallas.

It would be difficult (even for Texans) to exaggerate the impact that petroleum has had on the state's history, economy, politics, and educational institutions. What does the future hold, though? Geologists point out two disturbing realities. First, although three of the world's largest petroleum provinces lie entirely or partly within Texas, the size difference between the world's largest oil province (the Persian Gulf) and Texas' largest oil province (the Permian Basin) is enormous. Second, all the major Texas oil fields have become seriously depleted. Gone are the days when a single shallow well would gush 100,000 barrels per day. In fact, the main discovery phase for Texas petroleum reached its peak in the 1930s, almost sixty years ago. By the end of the 1950s, nearly all of the current fields, large and small, had been discovered, and the industry had passed into a production phase with ever-decreasing reserves.

Texas oil and gas production peaked in 1972 and has declined steadily ever since. In 1990, the state still produced over 672 million barrels of crude oil and condensate, but from nearly 189,000 wells. That's an average of only 9.3 barrels per well per day, and only 6 percent of these wells flow under their own pressure; the remainder have to be pumped.

Is all lost? Geologists of the Bureau of Economic Geology don't think so (Fisher and Galloway 1983). They prefer to view the production phase as divided into conventional and unconventional recovery periods. They point out that 156 billion barrels of oil have been discovered in Texas, and they anticipate that the total eventually will reach 176 billion barrels. Because only about 50 billion barrels have been produced, most of the state's oil is still in the ground. The problem, they contend, is that conventional recovery methods are only about 30 percent effective. Given that constraint, Texas oil fields are expected to yield only about 10 billion more barrels of crude. As things now stand, approximately two-thirds of the state's oil will be left in the ground!

With rewards so great and alternatives so bleak, Fisher and Galloway see us entering the age of the "sophisticated productionist"—one who combines all available geologic and engineering expertise to improve the current anemic recovery rate. They point to horizontal drilling as a good example. Oil in the Pearsall field of South Texas, for instance, is trapped in vertical rock fractures, few of which are intersected when conventional drilling is employed. By slowly diverting the drill bit to cut horizontally, many fractures are penetrated. The result has been some highly productive wells.

Although the Texas petroleum industry definitely has entered a new era, Texas remains the nation's leading petroleum producer. Moreover, untold potential natural gas may exist below salt beds of the Gulf of Mexico.

Coal

Petroleum still may be king in Texas, but prior to the availability of oil and gas, mines west of the Dallas–Fort Worth area, at Bridgeport, Newcastle, Strawn, and Thurber, produced significant amounts of bituminous coal. These North-Central Texas mines extracted Paleozoic (Pennsylvanian) age coal, and coal also is found in Mesozoic (Cretaceous) rocks in the Trans-Pecos region of Texas and in the Eagle Pass–Piedras Negras area (*piedras negras* are black rocks). Lignite, however, now surpasses bituminous coal in economic importance. Lignite is a brownish-black low-grade coal that can be used when geologic and economic conditions are appropriate. Conditions in East Texas are appropriate. The Gulf Coastal Plain has plenty of lignite (fig. 7.5), and the electrical industry is using it to supply power to nearby urban centers. The Bureau of Economic Geology has published a number of lignite papers, but a short review by Kaiser (1978) provides the basic information on the geologic setting and exploitation of Texas lignite.

Texas lignite was produced as early as 1850 and was a major Texas energy resource until 1930, when the advent of abundant, inexpensive oil and natural gas produced a hiatus in lignite development. That period ended in the 1970s, when petroleum and natural gas supplies diminished and prices soared. Suddenly lignite became competitive again, at least as an energy source for steam-generated electrical power.

Texas lignite originated from compressed and coalified plant material laid down some fifty million years ago (Eocene) in several early Cenozoic Gulf Coastal Plain formations. The organic material was deposited in ancient river, delta, and coastal lagoon environments. Most of the

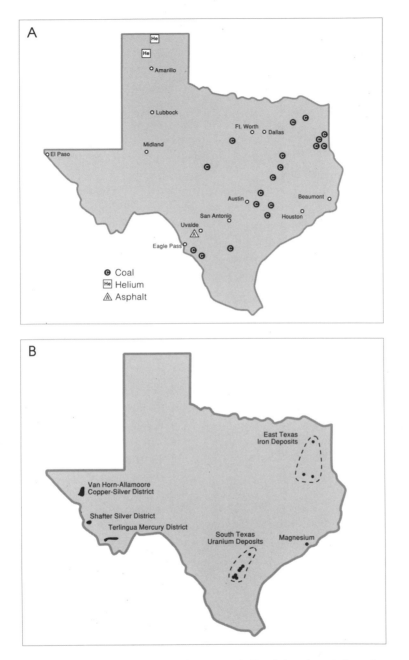

FIG. 7.5. Some natural resources of Texas, including (A) coal, asphalt, and helium; and (B) various metals.

Map by Nancy Place; adapted from Kier et al. (1977) and Garner et al. (1979).

known near-surface lignite is found in rocks of the Wilcox Group. Wilcox rocks crop out in a band running just east of the cities of Dallas, Austin, and San Antonio, although very little lignite is mined south of Austin (fig. 7.5). Near Longview, about twenty miles west of Marshall, large drag-lines with gigantic buckets are used to mine lignite. Lignite is also mined near Winfield, along Interstate Highway 30 between Dallas and Texarkana. The lignite is burned to generate electricity for the Dallas–Fort Worth area.

Lignite is mined using stripping methods. Only seams greater than 3 feet thick can be profitably mined, but a ten-foot lignite seam is considered exceptional. The overburden is removed, and the lignite extracted. Mining depths usually do not exceed 120 feet. The overburden is then replaced and the surface revegetated, mostly to woodland in the north and pasture land in the south.

Asphalt

Asphalt is a common paving material produced from petroleum, but Texas has places were natural asphalt is found. It formed when crude oil came close to Earth's surface and the more volatile components evaporated. To stand in an asphalt quarry is to be surrounded by the source rock for some ancient oil field. Tar permeates the porous, fossil-rich rock like an environmental geologist's nightmare, but tar and rock here are found in just the right proportions to be quarried, crushed, and used for pavement. The largest natural asphalt mines in Texas are found near the small Uvalde County towns of Cline and Blewett (fig. 7.5 and fig. 7.6).

Helium

Early oil-field workers are reported to have amazed their buddies by nonchalantly putting a flame to gas escaping from some Panhandle wells. When the expected fatal explosion failed to occur, they would yell after their fast-retreating former friends that the escaping gas was noncombustible helium. (Note: Don't try this at home!)

Helium is not a fossil fuel, but it is mixed with the natural gas produced in the Texas Panhandle from Amarillo northward. Helium extraction plants are located north of Amarillo at Masterson and Dumas, and in Hansford County on the Oklahoma border (fig. 7.5). The federal government has a helium storage facility at the Cliffside Field near Amarillo, where industries stockpile extra helium produced during the winter heating season.

FIG. 7.6. An asphalt quarry near Uvalde, showing dark, asphalt-rich layers in limestone. Photograph by author.

It is common knowledge that helium floats balloons and blimps, but most helium is used for other purposes. As the oil-field tricksters demonstrated, helium will not burn, a property that makes it ideal for lighter-than-air ships and for use as an inert gas shield in arc welding. The National Aeronautics and Space Administration (NASA) sends helium-filled balloons into the upper atmosphere above its research facility at Palestine, Texas, and uses large volumes of helium to pressurize and purge the tanks of its space shuttles. At ordinary pressures, helium cannot be solidified but rather remains liquid down to absolute zero. Helium evaporates at −269 degrees Celsius, a full 73 degrees lower than liquid nitrogen. Some materials become superconducting when immersed in liquid helium, producing mighty magnetic fields with a fraction of the energy required by conventional electromagnets. Hospitals use liquid helium for magnetic resonance imaging (MRI), a powerful new diagnostic tool. Helium's inert nature makes it breathable, and a mixture of 80 percent helium and 20 percent oxygen is used as an artificial atmosphere for divers working under high pressure. Normal atmosphere is nitrogen-rich, and nitrogen under high pressure dissolves in the blood, where it is toxic; helium only makes you sound like Donald Duck.

Industrial Rocks and Minerals

I often wonder why anthropologists go to such extremes in searching for the remains of Stone Age people, the Neanderthals. In fact, according to Bates and Jackson's delightful book *The Modern Stone Age* (1982), we are all Neanderthals, because we live in a Stone Age.

These authors point out that people today are far more dependent on "stones" than their prehistoric ancestors ever were. The mining geologists like to say, "If you can't grow it, it has to be mined." Each year, for every person in the United States, an average of over eleven tons of rock is processed, merely to produce the things the modern lifestyle demands. Stone products pave streets, insulate homes, and go into glass, paper, soap—indeed, into almost everything, including the kitchen sink. Modern agriculture would not be possible without the use of fertilizers and pesticides derived, in part, from rock.

Almost all the key nonfuel commodities are industrial minerals. In descending order of economic importance, they are: portland cement, stone, magnesium, sulfur, sand and gravel, salt, lime, gypsum, and clay. Texas also has produced smaller amounts of the following nonmetallic commodities, listed alphabetically: abrasives, agate, agricultural limestone, asphaltic limestone, barite, brick, brine, caliche, fluorspar, gems, graphite, helium, hydrogen sulfide, iron ore, lightweight aggregates, lignite, marble, mica, perlite, serpentine, soapstone, sodium hydroxide, sodium sulfate, sulfuric acid, talc, uranium, vermiculite, and at least twenty different metals besides.

This chapter concentrates on several of the more interesting metals and the industrial rocks and minerals most important economically.

Portland Cement

"Take four parts crushed limestone and one part clay or shale, season lightly with sandstone or iron, mix and grind, bake at 2,600 degrees Fahrenheit, and allow to cool. Add a dash of gypsum and grind very fine." Since its patenting by Joseph Aspidin in 1824, that's been the approximate recipe for a mud pie called portland cement because of its resemblance to Portland Stone, a building stone widely used in Great Britain.

Portland cement is the Lone Star State's leading nonfuel mineral product. Texas has about eleven cement plants, mostly located at rock sources near the urban centers of Dallas–Fort Worth, Austin, and San Antonio. It's not glamorous, but cement worth about $300 million is produced each year. Texas historically has accounted for about 10 percent of the total annual U.S. cement production and in recent years has ranked second only to California.

Gypsum

Texas ranks fourth among the states in production of crude gypsum, second in output of calcined (heated in a kiln) gypsum, and first in gypsum recovered as waste from other processes. Gypsum rock is produced from a number of quarries in Central and North-Central Texas. Uncalcined gypsum is used to control the setting time of portland cement. It is also widely used as a sulfur additive to soil. Calcined gypsum is used mostly in the manufacture of wallboard and plaster. Texas certainly has no shortage of gypsum. About six hundred square miles of Culberson County is underlain by a gypsum bed up to sixty-five feet thick.

Crushed Rock

Texas ranks third among the states in production of crushed stone, and 93 percent of the state's crushed stone is derived from limestone exposed along the Balcones Escarpment. Most crushed limestone is used to provide a firm foundation for roads and buildings. Basalt, also known as traprock, is crushed to provide a base for railroad tracks, and a small amount of crushed marble is used to make terrazzo floors and countertops. Ordinary crushed limestone is the most abundant component of portland cement.

Very pure limestone ($CaCO_3$) is heated in a kiln to drive off the carbon dioxide and produce lime. Lime is used as a flux in steel manufacturing, in sewage treatment, and in making paper, glass, and many other products. Lime also is used on cropland, both as a nutrient and to neutralize acidic soil. Lime can turn clay-rich, plastic soil into a hard and durable material. About 300,000 tons of lime were used for this purpose beneath pavement and buildings of the Dallas–Fort Worth Airport.

Sand, Gravel, and Clay

For each U.S. resident, an average of about five tons of sand, gravel, and clay are used annually. Sand and gravel combine with cement to make the artificial rock, concrete. Constructing an average new house requires fifty tons of concrete aggregate, an individual's quota for ten years, and the average mile of four-lane highway requires eighty-five thousand tons (an individual's quota for seventeen thousand years).

Clay is used to make bricks, tile, pottery, and drilling mud; and it is used as a filler in numerous products—fertilizer, for example. Some clays make fine china, and clay gives the gloss to the slick paper in magazines. Texas ranks third in clay production, producing a variety of clays (e.g., ball clays, bentonite, common clay, shale, fire clay, fuller's earth, and kaolin) from pits in North Texas, from counties surrounding the Dallas–Fort Worth area, from Bastrop and Guadalupe counties east of Austin and San Antonio, and from Fort Bend County south of the Houston area.

Dimension Stone

Dimension stone is natural rock material quarried and cut into shapes that have specified dimensions. Granite and limestone are by far the most abundant source rock for dimension stone, but a little sandstone and marble is produced from time to time (Garner 1992). Granite is produced from rock of Precambrian age in Burnet, Gillespie, Llano, and Mason counties (fig. 7.7). Limestone is quarried from Permian rock in Jones and Shackelford counties north of Abilene, and from Cretaceous rock in Travis and Williamson counties near Austin. The limestone from Travis and Williamson counties comes from the Walnut Formation in two distinctive types. One is a fine to medium cross-bedded limestone marketed as Cordova Cream. The other is Cordova Shell, a striking rock from which shells have been dissolved, leaving shell-shaped voids. Both types are widespread in structures found in Texas and across the nation. Red Triassic sandstone was quarried recently in Ward County at the southern edge of the Southern High Plains to refurbish the Bexar County courthouse, but no Central Texas marble has been produced since 1980.

Salt and Sodium Sulfate

From ancient times to the present day, salt has remained one of the world's most heavily traded minerals. It accounts for approximately two-thirds of the world's seaborne mineral trade. Salt is used as a food seasoning and for highway de-icing. Salt by itself, or the sodium and

Fig. 7.7. A granite quarry near Marble Falls.
Courtesy *Texas Highways*.

chlorine it contains, have about fourteen thousand identified uses. The United States is the world's largest salt-producing nation, and Texas produces about one-fifth of the nation's salt. Still, Louisiana produces almost twice as much, making Texas the second-ranking producer state.

Dow Chemical, the largest producer of salt in Texas, extracts brine from beneath Brazoria County south of Houston; and Morton has an underground mine and brine wells in Van Zandt County east of Dallas (fig. 7.8). Other firms extract salt in Chambers, Duval, Ector, Fort Bend, Harris, Jefferson, and Matagorda counties. Salt domes—tall columns of salt that have risen tens of thousands of feet from salt beds below—are the source of most of the salt. Hundreds of domes are known in the Texas-Louisiana section of the Gulf Coast, but only a few need be mined to meet all our salt needs. Salt at some domes is mined underground as rock salt; at other domes, it is dissolved and extracted as brine.

Salt is not the only product of economic interest in domes, and domes are not the only source of salt. Some domes also produce petroleum and sulfur, and bedded salt is found along with other evaporite minerals beneath parts of West Texas and adjacent New Mexico. West Texas salt is produced in Ector County, and sodium sulfate is extracted from brine pumped from below the Panhandle town of Seagraves. Sodium sulfate is used in the manufacture of paper and is of increasing importance in laundry detergents as a replacement for phosphate. Texas currently ranks second among three sodium sulfate-producing states.

Fɪɢ. 7.8. Underground in the Grand Saline salt dome.
Courtesy Morton Salt, Morton International, Inc.

Sulfur

Brimstone, "the stone that burns"—that's sulfur. Elemental sulfur is a common substance in the caprock on Texas salt domes (fig. 7.2). It occurs there as bright yellow grains and crystals, along with the minerals calcite (calcium carbonate) and anhydrite (calcium sulfate). Anhydrite appears to be the ultimate source for the sulfur; anaerobic bacteria living in the dome seem to free sulfur from anhydrite as they metabolize anhydrite's oxygen and "spit out" its sulfur.

About 85 percent of all sulfur mined is converted to sulfuric acid, the most abundantly used mineral acid. Tremendous quantities of sulfuric acid are used in the conversion of phosphate rock to phosphate in fertilizer (the middle number on the fertilizer bag) and in the leaching of copper from copper ore. Sulfuric acid also is used in vulcanization of natural rubber and in the making of paints, rayon, film, paper, dyes, fungicides, and thousands of other products. Three hundred pounds of

FIG. 7.9. A sulfur operation along the Texas Gulf Coast.
Courtesy *Texas Highways*.

sulfuric acid are "consumed" each year by industry on behalf of each
of us.

Sulfur melts at only 235 degrees Fahrenheit—a fact that didn't escape
Herman Frasch, the German-born American who in 1895 invented the
Frasch process for sulfur recovery. Pressurized water is heated to above
the melting point of sulfur and pumped below to melt sulfur. Molten
sulfur has twice the specific gravity of water, so it sinks to form pools,
which are then pumped to the surface. The molten sulfur generally is allowed to cool in great blocks which are later broken, loaded, and shipped
(fig. 7.9). Frasch sulfur is extracted from Boling Dome southwest of
Houston and from bedded deposits in the West Texas counties of Pecos
and Culberson.

Sulfur is removed as an unwanted component in natural gas and
crude oil. In addition, sulfuric acid, the largest end use of sulfur, is a by-
product recovered during the smelting of sulfide ores of copper, lead,
and zinc. Between Frasch sulfur and sulfur recovered during petroleum
refining, Texas is the nation's leading producer.

"One person's treasure is another person's trash." Sulfur in the form
of sulfur dioxide contributes to the serious environmental problem of
acid rain. The largest source of acid rain is sulfur produced by burning

fossil fuels and by smelting metallic sulfide ores. The challenge is to take the sulfur from fuels and ores and put it to use in the manufacture of the thousands of commercial products that are part of our modern lives, without injecting it into the atmosphere and sprinkling it over forests and lakes.

Metals

Smelters and refineries located at Dallas, El Paso, Laredo, and along the Gulf Coast cause the official list of metals produced in Texas to be fairly long. From A to Z, they include: aluminum, antimony, cadmium, copper, gold, iron, lead, magnesium, manganese, molybdenum, palladium, platinum, rare-earth elements, selenium, silver, tin, tungsten, vanadium, and zinc.

In reality, metal mining in Texas is almost nonexistent; nor has production been particularly great historically. Only iron, magnesium, and uranium have been produced recently in Texas; copper, gold, lead, mercury, silver, and zinc have had only very modest historic production. Surprisingly, Texas metals do not come from veins associated with Trans-Pecos igneous rocks or even from the promising-sounding Central Mineral Region. Nearly all of the recent metal production has come from the Texas Gulf Coastal Plain or from the Gulf water itself. Iron has been mined from sedimentary rocks of the northern Gulf Coastal Plain, and uranium is extracted from sedimentary rocks to the south. Gulf water yields magnesium compounds via the Dow Chemical Company plant in Brazoria County. Here let us consider the three most recently produced metals and three others of significant historic interest.

Magnesium

Magnesium is the third most abundant element dissolved in sea water (0.13 percent), well behind sodium and chlorine. Dow's Freeport plant (fig 7.5) extracts hydrous magnesium chloride from seawater and then produces magnesium metal by electrolysis. Magnesium is used to desulfurize and strengthen iron and steel, and as an alloy with aluminum. Magnesium alloys can be die-cast, and they shield against electromagnetic interference, a property that makes them useful as housing for electronic equipment.

Iron

Iron has been mined in Texas since 1855 from very low-grade iron ores located in early Cenozoic sedimentary rocks of East Texas (fig. 7.5) (Eckel 1938). One of the earliest furnaces was located at Rusk in Cherokee County. The site was chosen as the location for a state penitentiary, and convicts were supposed to process the local iron ore into steel. Operations started in 1884 but ceased in 1909. The facility eventually was converted into a state psychiatric hospital.

Lone Star Steel, located at Lone Star, eight-five miles north of Rusk, made a somewhat better attempt at smelting the low-grade iron ore. Ore was removed by dragline from open pits, upgraded at a beneficiation plant, upgraded further with iron-ore pellets transported from a "real" iron deposit, and fed into one of five open-hearth furnaces. Recently, hard times in the steel industry also have forced Lone Star Steel to close.

The ore minerals in these East Texas deposits consist of secondary iron oxides, hydroxides, and carbonates, but the original source of the iron is believed to have been grains of a greenish mineral called glauconite. Glauconite is an iron-rich mineral formed by a chemical reaction between sea water and the fecal material of marine organisms.

Uranium

Uranium was discovered in Karnes County in 1954, as a result of an airborne radiometric survey (fig. 7.5). Open-pit uranium mining began in 1961, and leach-mining was added in 1975. The information below comes from *South Texas Uranium Province* (Galloway et al. 1979), one of several publications offering overviews of the South Texas uranium province.

The original source of the uranium is believed to be Trans-Pecos volcanic ash and volcanic rock fragments eroded and mixed in with Gulf Coastal Plain sediments. Uranium is readily leached from volcanic material by oxygen-rich ground water and is then transported down the hydrologic gradient. If uranium-rich ground water encounters a reducing environment, the uranium is precipitated in any available rock pore space. Reducing environments may be caused by an abundance of organic material, petroleum seeps along faults, or an abundance of sulfide minerals in the sediment. In general, South Texas uranium deposits are low grade. Recently, competition from foreign sources, combined with reduced demand for uranium, has brought the Texas uranium industry near closing.

Mercury

Although the mines are no longer active, Texas is better known for its mercury deposits than for ore deposits of any other metal (Sharpe 1980). Most of the production has come from the Terlingua district west of Big Bend National Park (fig. 7.5). The district proper extends in a belt five miles wide, from Study Butte to near Lajitas on the Rio Grande, a distance of about sixteen miles (fig. 7.10). Bright red cinnabar (mercury sulfide) was first used in war paint by Comanche Indians and later became the chief ore mineral for mercury. Mining companies obtain mercury simply by heating the cinnabar to about 350 degrees Fahrenheit. Heating drives off mercury vapor, which is then cooled, condensed to a liquid, and bottled in seventy-six-pound steel cylinders called flasks. Mercury fulminate was used in wartime blasting caps and bullet primers. Mercury is also a catalyst for making chlorine and caustic soda, and it has been used in thermometers, switches, and batteries. It is useful in gold extraction.

Mining for mercury began at Terlingua in 1894, and the mines were worked continuously until 1946. At one time, two thousand people worked the mines and processing plant, and the Terlingua mines were one of the most important sources of mercury in the U.S. More than 150,000 flasks of mercury have been produced from the southern part of Trans-Pecos Texas. Two-thirds of that total has come from Terlingua's Chisos Mine, which operated almost continuously from 1902 to 1937, leaving behind nearly twenty-three miles of underground workings. Mining activity in the Terlingua district has been shut down completely since the early 1970s, but seething pots of red material, lethal vapors, and more than a few flasks still can be seen at Terlingua's annual chili cook-off.

Gold and Silver

Periodically a story circulates about a lost Spanish mine or a discovery of gold, silver, or platinum somewhere in Texas. Are these discoveries real? Are there precious metals in Texas?

A few years back, newspapers were carrying reports of gold found near Uvalde. I asked an economic geologist friend from Nevada if he had heard about it. "Everyone in the industry has heard about it," he replied, "and everybody's laughing."

Another fellow who spent time in real gold country put it this way. "A gold mine," claimed Mark Twain, "is a hole in the ground with a liar at the top."

Fɪɢ. 7.10. An abandoned mercury mine shaft and headframe at
Study Butte. Courtesy *Texas Highways.*

No Texas platinum discoveries ever have been authenticated, and gold has been found only in very small amounts. Silver has shown more promise. The sober truth, however, Evans (1975) concludes, is that "the story of gold and silver in Texas [is] a story more of sweat than reward, more of hope than fact."

The major exceptions to Evans' bleak appraisal are the Presidio Mine, near Shafter in far West Texas, and the Hazel Mine, north of Van Horn (fig. 7.5). Evans puts it this way: "Precious-metal production can be expressed in just two words—Presidio and Hazel."

Gold, silver, and some lead are found in the Shafter district, located on the south flank of the Chinati Mountains, overlooking the Rio Grande Valley and the border towns of Presidio and Ojinaga. Presidio is also the name of the district's and the state's major historic precious-metal mine. The Presidio Mine opened in the 1880s and was active until 1942. During that time it is believed to have yielded more than 92 percent of the state's total silver production and at least 73 percent of Texas' total production of gold.

Most of the rest of the state's silver and gold production has come from the Van Horn–Allamoore mining district, located north of Interstate Highway 10, just west of Van Horn (fig. 7.5) (Price et al. 1985). Copper-silver ore is found there, along and near fractures cutting Precambrian, Paleozoic, and Mesozoic rocks. The most productive deposit is the Hazel Mine. It is reported to have been discovered in 1856 and operated sporadically until closing in 1947. The small amount of precious metal not produced by the Hazel and Presidio mines has come from small deposits in the Quitman Mountains of West Texas and from the Central Mineral Region.

The name Central Mineral Region must have been applied more in accord with hope than reality. The area contains the state's largest exposures of Precambrian rocks, and much has been expected of them. These rocks have been seriously prospected for asbestos, barite, bismuth, chromite, copper, feldspar, fluorite, gem topaz, gold, granite, graphite, iron ore, lead, magnesite, manganese, molybdenum, quartz, rare-earth minerals, serpentine, silver, soapstone, tin, tungsten, uranium, and vermiculite, but they consistently produce only granite.

Legends and rumors of lost gold mines abound in this country, but the only documented gold production has come from the Heath Mine, located five miles northeast of Llano. The mine was discovered by accident in the early 1890s and was worked briefly from 1896 to 1899. While there are more myths than mines in the Central Mineral Region, it is true that placer gold may be panned in very small amounts from several area streams, particularly the Little Llano River and Sandy Creek.

References

Bates, R. L., and J. A. Jackson. 1982. *Our modern stone age.* Los Altos, Calif.: William Kaufmann. 125p.

Clark, J. A. 1952. *Spindletop.* New York: Random House. 306p.

Clark, J. A., and M. T. Halbouty. 1972. *The last boom.* New York: Random House. 305p.

Eckel, E. 1938. *The brown ores of eastern Texas.* United States Geological Survey Bulletin 902. Washington, D.C.: United States Government Printing Office. 157p.

Evans, T. J. 1975. *Gold and silver in Texas.* Mineral Resource Circular No. 56. Austin: Bureau of Economic Geology, University of Texas at Austin. 35p.

Fisher, W., and W. Galloway. 1983. *Potential for additional oil recovery in*

Texas. Geological Circular 83-2. Austin: Bureau of Economic Geology, University of Texas at Austin. 20p.

Galloway, W.; T. Ewing; C. Garrett; N. Tyler; and D. Bebout. 1983. *Atlas of major Texas oil reservoirs.* Austin: Bureau of Economic Geology, University of Texas at Austin. 139p.

Galloway, W.; A. Finley; and C. Henry. 1979. *South Texas Uranium Province: geologic perspective.* Guidebook 18. Austin: Bureau of Economic Geology, University of Texas at Austin. 81p.

Garner, E. L. 1992. *The dimension stone industry of Texas.* Mineral Resource Circular No. 82. Bureau of Economic Geology, University of Texas at Austin. 16p.

Garner, E. L.; A. E. St. Clair; and T. J. Evans. 1979, reprinted 1987. *Mineral resources of Texas.* Map. Austin: Bureau of Economic Geology, University of Texas at Austin. 1 sheet. 1:1,000,000 scale.

Kaiser, W. 1978. *Electric power generation from Texas lignite.* Geological Circular 78-3. Austin: Bureau of Economic Geology, University of Texas at Austin. 18p.

Kier, R. S.; L. E. Garner; and L. F. Brown, Jr. 1977. *Land Resources of Texas.* Austin: Bureau of Economic Geology, University of Texas at Austin. 42p., 1 map.

McBride, M. W., and A. L. Dobbs. 1983. *Nonpetroleum mineral producers in Texas.* 1983. Mineral Resource Circular No. 74. Austin: Bureau of Economic Geology, University of Texas at Austin. 94p.

Price, J.; C. Henry; A. Standen; and J. Posey. 1985. *Origin of silver-copper-lead deposits in red-bed sequences of Trans-Pecos Texas: Tertiary mineralization in Precambrian, Permian, and Cretaceous sandstone.* Report of Investigations No. 145. Austin: Bureau of Economic Geology, University of Texas at Austin. 65p.

Sharpe, Roger D. 1980. *Development of the mercury mining industry: Trans-Pecos Texas.* Mineral Resource Circular No. 64. Austin: Bureau of Economic Geology, University of Texas at Austin. 32p.

8   Texas Ground Water and Caves

A nation that fails to plan intelligently for the development and
protection of its precious waters will be condemned to wither because
of its shortsightedness.
—U.S. President Lyndon B. Johnson, 1968

Surface and Ground Water

"Texas has two kinds of water," drawled the farmer. "Too damn
much and too damn little." For the hydrogeologist, however, the two
main kinds of water are surface water and ground water.

Texas surface water includes some 11,247 named rivers and streams
with a combined length of about eighty thousand miles. The total average annual runoff (streamflow) is estimated at 49 million acre-feet.
(Note: An acre-foot is the amount of water needed to cover an acre to a
depth of one foot. An acre-foot equals 325,857 gallons or 43,560 cubic
feet.) In addition, there is an enormous amount of surface water—about
60 million acre-feet—in the state's 5,700 lakes and reservoirs (fig. 8.1).
Minnesota, with 4,854 square miles of inland water, may have the most
of any state; but Texas, with 4,790 square miles of lakes and reservoirs,
ranks a close second. Important as surface water may be for the Texas
economy, it is only the second most important source of water for Texas.

Most of the fresh water in Texas is contained in unconsolidated sediment and porous, permeable rock formations known as *aquifers.* Important aquifers underlie approximately 76 percent of the state and have
a conservatively estimated total capacity of about 9 billion acre-feet of
potable water.

The Texas Water Development Board estimated that Texans in 1984
used 8,854,470 acre-feet of ground water, an enormous sum but less
than one-tenth of one percent of the water stored underground. Of all
water pumped, 78 percent was used for irrigation, and irrigating the
High Plains accounted for a whopping 60 percent of the total use. Mu-
nicipalities consumed 17 percent of the water, although most of that also
was used for irrigation—watering the suburban lawns of the crabgrass

126

FIG. 8.1. Lake Amistad on the Texas border with Mexico. Courtesy *Texas Highways*.

frontier. A significant percentage of the total municipal ground water pumpage occurred in the Houston and San Antonio areas. Of the remaining 5 percent, 2 percent went for manufacturing and 1 percent each for livestock, electrical generation, and mining.

Major aquifers are defined as those that yield large quantities of water and underlie comparatively large areas of the state. Minor aquifers are defined as either yielding large quantities of water in a relatively small area or as yielding relatively small quantities of water in a large part of the state. A total of seven major and seventeen minor aquifers have been delineated in Texas. Some characteristics of the major aquifers are listed in table 8.1, and their distribution is shown on figure 8.2.

Now let's take a more detailed look at the major Texas aquifers and see what most Texans are drinking.

High Plains Aquifer

The High Plains or Ogallala Aquifer underlies all or part of forty-six Texas Panhandle counties (fig. 8.2). The aquifer consists mostly of the Ogallala Formation, formed during Cenozoic time from gravel, sand, silt, and clay shed from mountains to the west. Its maximum thickness, almost nine hundred feet, is in Ochiltree County. Ground water flows southeastward through the aquifer, toward the eastern caprock escarpment of the High Plains.

The High Plains Aquifer is not without its water problems. High concentrations of chloride, sulfate, and nitrate are found in water of the southern part of the Panhandle. Possible reasons include dissolution of underlying salt beds, local contamination from petroleum production, contamination from animal feed lots, and leaching of nitrogen-based fertilizers applied to croplands. High arsenic concentrations in some

Table 8.1 Major Texas Aquifers: Their Geologic Age and Characteristics

Major Aquifers	Geologic Units	Lithologic Properties
High Plains (Ogallala)	Ogallala Formation; Cenozoic age	0–900 feet of unconsolidated, sand, silt, clay, and gravel, with some caliche beds
Trinity	Trinity Group; Cretaceous age	100–1,200 feet of sand, silt, clay, and shale; with some limestone
Edwards	Georgetown Formation, Edwards Group, and Comanche Peak Formation; Cretaceous age	350–600 feet of massive to thin-bedded and locally cavernous limestone and dolomite
Gulf Coast	Various units of Mid-Cenozoic to recent age	500–3,200 feet of sand, silt, gravel, and clay
Edwards-Trinity	Georgetown Formation, Edwards Group, and Comanche Peak Formation Cretaceous age	0–800 feet of cavernous limestone with some sand, silt, and clay
Carrizo-Wilcox	Carrizo Formation and Wilcox Group; Early Cenozoic age	150–3,000 feet of iron-rich sand with clay, silt, and gravel
Alluvium and Bolson Deposits	Various units; Cenozoic to recent age	0–9,000 feet of unconsolidated to poorly consolidated silt, sand, gravel, and clay

Source: Texas Water Commission (1989).

areas also may be related to agricultural activity. Almost 20 percent of the High Plains water samples are exceedingly high in fluoride. Fluoride in small quantities taken during the enamel forming process reduces tooth decay, but fluoride in excessive concentrations can cause discoloration and mottling of teeth.

Perhaps the most vexing High Plains water problem is that Ogallala water appears to be going the way of the mammoths and saber-toothed cats who once made their homes on this range. The vast amount of water

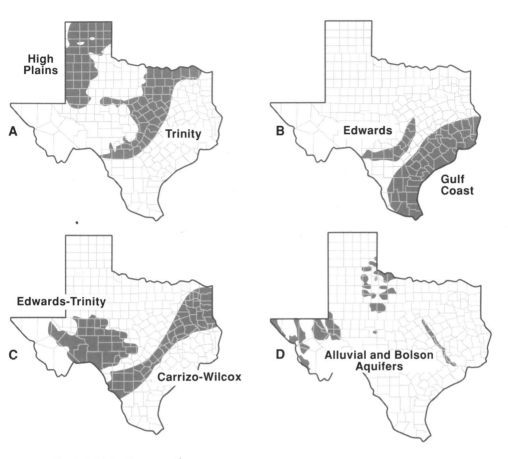

Fig. 8.2. Major Texas aquifers.
Map by Nancy Place; adapted from Texas Water Commission (1989).

contained in this aquifer accumulated there long before the coming of settlers. It is, in fact, largely the result of higher rainfall during the Ice Age. Erosion of the Pecos River Valley has isolated the Ogallala Formation from ground water derived from the Rockies, denying it that source of recharge. Today's low annual precipitation and high evaporation rate produce an estimated effective recharge rate of less than 0.2 inches per year, just a small fraction of the annual withdrawal. Ogallala water, then, is, in effect, being mined. When the "ore" is gone, large tracts of land will either have to go out of production or revert to dryland farming practices.

Fɪɢ. 8.3. Highly permeable rock of the Edwards Aquifer. Photo by author.

Even the Internal Revenue Service has recognized that Panhandle real estate without water for irrigation has a lower value and has allowed farmers there to depreciate their land as the water table drops.

Trinity Aquifer

The Trinity Aquifer provides water for public, domestic, industrial, and agricultural purposes in fifty-six counties northwest of the Balcones and the Luling-Mexia-Talco fault zones (fig. 8.2). Trinity Group rocks consist of the Paluxy, Glen Rose, and Travis Peak formations, all Cretaceous sedimentary formations deposited in a coastal or shallow marine environment. Water quality, in terms of total dissolved solids, decreases eastward. Excessive pumping in the Dallas–Fort Worth area has caused the water levels there to decline and may be causing poorer quality eastern water to be drawn below this major urban center. Oil and gas production, with its associated disposal of salt water, has been suggested as a possible source of high ground-water salinity in parts of Grayson and Collin counties in the far northern part of the aquifer.

Edwards Aquifer

The Edwards Aquifer parallels the Balcones Fault zone and covers a large area of Central and South-Central Texas (fig. 8.2). It consists mostly of limestone of the Edwards Group, which contains layers of porous—even cavernous—rock created by limestone dissolution (fig. 8.3).

Fɪɢ. 8.4. Barton Springs at Austin's Zilker Park is a major discharge point of the Edwards Aquifer. Photo by author.

The extremely high permeability of these layers produces some of the most prolific water wells in the world. The Edwards limestone is exposed along the Balcones Fault zone, where it receives surface recharge mainly from streams that flow across the region during floods.

The cavernous Edwards limestone allows for swift, underground movement of water movement. Water levels in San Antonio wells may jump ten feet or more in a single day following heavy rain on the recharge zone. The water doesn't actually flow to San Antonio in one day, but water in the wells rises as a result of increased hydraulic pressure applied at the recharge zone, much as pouring water in one end of a U-shaped tube causes water at the other end to rise. Water flows through the aquifer from the recharge area to major pumping points in the region and to natural discharge points at springs such as Leona Springs near Uvalde, San Pedro and San Antonio springs in San Antonio, Comal Springs in New Braunfels, San Marcos Springs at San Marcos, Barton Springs in Austin (fig. 8.4), and Salado Springs in Salado.

Below the surface, the aquifer is overlain by impermeable Del Rio

Clay and underlain by the relatively impermeable Glen Rose Formation, which together make the Edwards a confined aquifer. Water in the confined zone is under some artesian pressure and, in places, rises to the surface in flowing artesian springs and wells. A spectacular example existed briefly at the Living Waters Catfish Farm fifteen miles southwest of downtown San Antonio. A thirty-inch well completed there in 1991 encountered, at a depth of 1,660 feet, a cavern containing pressurized water at 98 degrees Fahrenheit. That well and another on the property spouted between 30 and 50 million gallons daily, about a fourth the daily pumpage for all of San Antonio.

As with all limestone aquifers, hard-water problems exist, but in general the water quality is excellent. Locally high nitrate concentrations, probably from septic systems leaking into the aquifer, have been recorded from Edwards water. In addition, the extreme permeability that makes the Edwards aquifer such a prolific producer also makes it susceptible to contamination. The aquifer dips eastward toward the Gulf, and the water quality deteriorates concomitantly. The more saline water is attributed to dissolution of minerals from the rock and also may be the result of movement upward, along faults, of more saline water from greater depths.

Gulf Coast Aquifer

The Gulf Coast Aquifer covers all or parts of fifty-three counties flanking the Gulf Coast, from the Sabine River to the Rio Grande (fig 8.2). It is composed of late Cenozoic clay, silt, sand, and gravel, deposited under fluvial, deltaic, and shallow marine conditions. Individual rock units parallel the Gulf shoreline, dip toward the Gulf, and thicken dramatically as they dip. In densely populated areas, long-term ground water withdrawal has caused problems. Pumping in the Houston area, for example, has lowered the water table, allowing subsurface encroachment of salt water from beneath the Gulf of Mexico. Water withdrawal also has led to sediment compaction, land-surface subsidence, and flooding problems along the Gulf Coast (see chapter 10).

Edwards-Trinity Aquifer

Water-bearing Cretaceous sedimentary rocks underlie the Stockton Plateau east of the Pecos River and the Edwards Plateau from the Pecos River to the Central Mineral Region (fig. 8.2). The Edwards-Trinity Aquifer is used for irrigation and locally for municipal, industrial, livestock, and domestic purposes. Oil and gas is produced in the northwestern part of the region, where high chloride concentrations may be the result of past oil field brine disposal practices.

Carrizo-Wilcox Aquifer

The Carrizo-Wilcox Aquifer is one of the most extensive in Texas (fig. 8.2). Its sandstone furnishes water to all or parts of sixty-one counties in a belt extending from Arkansas and Louisiana to the Rio Grande. The Carrizo Formation and the underlying Wilcox Group were deposited in very early Cenozoic time (Eocene) from large rivers flowing to deltas at what was then the Texas coast. Gulfward tilting and erosion of coastal plain formations explain why the present-day outcrop pattern parallels the Gulf of Mexico. The aquifer is recharged directly by precipitation and from streams crossing the outcrop area. The aquifer yields water that is acceptable for most irrigation, municipal, and industrial uses along nearly all of its extent. Locally, water quality may be adversely affected by the smell of hydrogen sulfide or methane gas, or by an undesirable color due to lignite or excessive iron, especially in northeastern Texas.

Alluvial and Bolson Aquifers

Alluvial deposits consist of recently deposited, unconsolidated, streamborne sediment located along major Texas rivers. Bolson (basin-fill) deposits form in the mountainous parts of West Texas from sediment shed from the uplands into intermontane basins. Although geographically separate, these deposits have geologic and hydrologic similarities and are considered together as a single major aquifer (fig. 8.2).

Alluvium and bolson deposits are the major ground water source in far West Texas (fig. 8.5). Cenozoic alluvium is widespread in the upper part of the Pecos River Valley, and the Salt Bolson extends south from the Guadalupe Mountains in Culberson and Hudspeth counties. The Red Light Draw, Eagle Flat, and Green River Valley bolsons flank the Quitman and Eagle mountains of southern Hudspeth County, and the Presidio and Redford bolsons are a major source of water in the Rio Grande Valley near Presidio. In the El Paso area, large of amounts of ground water are drawn from the Mesilla Bolson west of the Franklin Mountains and from the Hueco Bolson to the east. In North-Central Texas, discontinuous alluvial beds support irrigation and towns over a twenty-three-county area, and a major source of water for irrigation in Southeast

Fɪɢ. 8.5. Irrigation from a bolson aquifer near Van Horn, Texas.
Courtesy *Texas Highways.*

Texas is a strip of alluvium two hundred miles long, flanking the Brazos River (fig. 8.2).

Caves and Caverns: The Work of Underground Water

The Texas Speleological Survey defines a *cave* as any natural cavity that is passable by humans and is either twenty-five feet long or longer, or fifteen feet deep or deeper (Veni 1988). To exclude such places as cliffside rock shelters, the survey further specifies that the entrance must be smaller than its length or depth.

Caves form in limestone when rainwater picks up atmospheric carbon dioxide and filters through decaying plants and soil to become slightly acidic. Acid ground water penetrates limestone and slowly, over hundreds of thousands of years, widens cavities, fractures, faults, and bedding planes to produce caves and caverns. As the surface above is removed by erosion and the water table drops below cave level, water drips through caves to produce stalactites, stalagmites, and columns. Eventually the roof of a cave may thin to the point of collapse, forming a sink-

FIG. 8.6. Devil's Sinkhole, now a state natural area near Rocksprings.
Courtesy *Texas Highways.*

hole (fig. 8.6). *Karst regions* are areas where sinkholes and caves are numerous, as in parts of Florida, the Mammoth Cave area of Kentucky, and around Carlsbad, New Mexico.

As we have seen, Texas has an abundant supply of limestone. The Lone Star State has, in fact, more caves than any other state. The total number is staggering. About three thousand have been documented, many more have been discovered but are not yet listed, and an untold number await discovery.

Speleologists are cave scientists. The down-to-earth folks who enjoy exploring the underworld usually refer to themselves simply as *cavers.* The word *cavern* generally is used to suggest a cave of considerable size. Commercial caves usually bill themselves as caverns (e.g., Caverns of Sonora or Carlsbad Caverns). The name of Mammoth Cave, however, suggests that no hard and fast rule applies. Particularly well-decorated caves are known as *show caves* or *pretties,* and Texas has some of the world's finest commercial caves (fig. 8.7 and table 8.2). The Caverns of Sonora, for example, are considered to be among the most beautifully decorated caves in the world. A past president of the National Speleological Society reportedly awarded it this accolade: "This is the most

FIG. 8.7. Natural Bridge Caverns. Courtesy *Texas Highways.*

indescribably beautiful cavern in the world. Its beauty cannot be exaggerated, even by Texans!"

The deepest cave in Texas is Sorcerer's Cave in Terrell County, a modest 525 feet from the highest to the lowest known level. The deepest known cave in the United States, however, is but a few miles from Texas. Carlsbad Cavern's giant neighbor in southern New Mexico, Lechuguilla Cave, is known to be at least 1,565 feet deep. Lechuguilla's vertical drop, however, can be considered petite compared to the 5,036-foot depth of the world's deepest known cave, in France. The longest known cave in Texas is Honey Creek Cave, north of San Antonio. About 19 miles of passages have been mapped, making it the twentieth longest cave in the U.S. and fiftieth in the world. The world's longest cave, the Mammoth Cave system in Kentucky, has over 330 miles of passages, and they are still counting. (Cave depths, lengths, and rankings are constantly changing as exploration continues.)

Limestone caverns are special places, full of mystery, beauty, and, for the inexperienced, danger. They attract the geologist to observe subterranean processes; the biologist for their special life forms; and the paleontologist, anthropologist, and archaeologist for clues to the past.

Cave Ecosystems

Caves have wondrous ecosystems in which a limited number of species share a rather restricted and resource-poor environment. To biologists, *troglobites* are organisms that spend their entire lives in caves. They show adaptations to their environment such as lost or reduced eyesight and pigmentation. They are distant relatives of surface creatures but have adapted to a new and unique environment.

Other creatures, such as bats, may spend their days in caves or hibernate there but emerge into the outside world on a regular schedule. During much of the year, bats issue forth in great swarms each evening to range as far as a hundred miles. Texas has more species of bats than any other state, thirty-three at latest count (Schmidly 1991 and Bryan 1993).

Bracken Cave, north of San Antonio, is the world's largest known remaining bat cave. On a good night, as many as 25 million (observers count the number of bat wings and divide by two) Mexican free-tail bats spew out of the entrance to roam far and wide before returning at dawn. After hanging around the cave all day, the bats are voracious. Each may consume as many as one hundred insects per hour, or one-third to one-half its own weight in a single night. Together the Bracken bats may consume up to three hundred thousand pounds of insects (the equivalent of over one hundred elephants) in a single night. There are an estimated 160 million bats on the Edwards Plateau. Bats from Bracken and other nearby caves feed in Central Texas for about 260 to 280 days per year, then, instead of hibernating, they spend the three coldest months in sunny Mexico.

Underground at Bracken Cave is a biologist's dream, but a nightmare for most of us. The temperature is about 100 degrees Fahrenheit, heated by the bodies of millions of bats. A caver can be overcome by ammonia fumes from bat droppings. Moreover, the cave floor is alive with beetles and worms waiting to devour any dying adult or baby bat that happens to fall to the floor.

Bat flights can be observed at Kickapoo Caverns near Del Rio, Devil's Sinkhole near Rocksprings, and Old Tunnel near Fredericksburg (Albright 1992). An enormous urban bat colony can be viewed at the Congress Street Bridge in Austin, and world-class Bracken Cave is being prepared both for its preservation and for public educational purposes.

Table 8.2　Commercial Caves of Texas

Cascade Caverns
Fourteen miles northwest of San Antonio on Interstate Highway 10 (exit 543), or
5 miles southeast of Boerne off U.S. Highway 87. Open since 1932, this cave features a 100-foot subterranean waterfall.

Cave Without a Name
Eleven miles northeast of Boerne, 6 miles via F.M. Road 474, then right 4.6 miles
on Kreutzberg Road. A contest to name the cave was won by a boy who said, "This
cave is too pretty to name." The cave has stalactites, stalagmites, and soda straws.

Caverns of Sonora
About 8 miles southwest of Sonora, off Interstate Highway 10 (exit 392) on F.M.
Road 1989. Considered to be one of the most beautifully decorated caves in the
world. An amazing profusion of delicate crystal growths and spectacular dripstone
formations, including rare helictites and soda straws. Temperature: 71 degrees
Fahrenheit.

Colorado Bend State Park
West of Lampasas, the park offers a tour of Gorman Cave. Reservations recommended.

Inner Space Caverns
Off Interstate Highway 35, 1 mile south of Georgetown or 27 miles north of Austin.
Cave formed by water-filled fractures along a limestone block of the Balcones
Fault system. The cave was discovered during construction of I-35 and is located
beneath the highway. The owners use lighting and acoustics to dramatize the
cave's natural beauty, and there is an inclined rail "subway" entrance. The cave
holds Ice-Age mammal fossils. Temperature: 72 degrees Fahrenheit.

Kickapoo Cavern State Park
Between Del Rio and Uvalde, 23 miles north of Brackettville on F.M. Road 674.
Green Cave, 2,000 feet long, is home to about one million Mexican free-tail bats.

Longhorn Cavern State Park
About 12 miles southeast of Buchanan Dam, 11 miles southwest of Burnet on
Park Road 4, or 6 miles off U.S. Highway 281. Officially opened in 1932, the cave
is on Backbone Ridge, one of a number of fault-block "mountains" in the Central

Mineral Region. Prehistoric inhabitants leaving their bones in the cave include a grizzly bear, bobcat, elephant, and bison. Two human skeletons, believed to be the remains of an Indian and a Confederate soldier, have been found. The cave is of historic interest as a secret Confederate gunpowder manufacturing site. Temperature: 64 degrees Fahrenheit.

Natural Bridge Caverns
Between San Antonio and New Braunfels. From Interstate Highway 10 or U.S. Highway 281 via Texas Highway 46 and F.M. Road 3009. From Interstate Highway 35 via F.M. Road 3009. This cave, now a U.S. National Landmark, was discovered in 1960 and named for a 60-foot natural limestone bridge at the entrance. The cave is nicely decorated and features large rooms. An underground stream is called Purgatory Creek. Temperature: 70 degrees Fahrenheit.

Wonder World Caverns
Bishop Street within the city of San Marcos. Discovered in 1893 and proclaiming itself as an earthquake-formed cave. Like Inner Space Caverns, the cave formed along the Balcones Fault system

---

Caves as Time Capsules

Because things may be preserved in a cave that would be destroyed almost anywhere else, caves can add greatly to our knowledge of the past. The skull of that earliest of cavers, Neanderthal Man, when found in a German cave in 1856, lent weight to arguments being advanced by Charles Darwin concerning the origin of species via natural selection. Somewhat later, twenty-five thousand years ago, cave dwellers left tools and cave "paintings" in northern Spain and southern France. Quite unintentionally, these early European ancestors reached across the ages to tell us, using soot and ocher, something about their world. Elsewhere, fragile personal items such as baskets and clothing have been preserved in caves as clues to how our ancient ancestors lived. Rock shelters along the Pecos River near Langtry contain paintings believed to be about nine thousand years old.

Fossils, especially the fossil bones of large vertebrates, commonly are found in caves. These animals may have lived in the caves, as bears did, or they may have wandered in, become lost in the darkness, and fallen to their deaths. If you've checked table 8.2, you may have wondered about those bison and elephant bones found in Longhorn Cavern. They could have been washed there by floods, or they could have been dragged in by bears or saber-toothed tigers. Friesenhahn Cave, near San Antonio, produced a large number of bones, including amphibians, reptiles, birds, and mammals. These fossils give a glimpse into life there about twenty thousand years ago. The cave apparently was the den of saber-toothed cats, because the bones of kittens, perhaps drowned in a flood, were found in this prehistoric den. Also found were the bones of a large number of immature mammoths, evidently an item high on the menu for cats of that day.

Caves and the Environment

In addition to their importance to the biological environment, sinkholes and cave systems are components of some of the most important aquifers of the state. Sinkholes commonly lead to cave systems and are important points of aquifer recharge. In the past, some sinkholes have been considered convenient locations for all sorts of refuse. Other sinkhole entrances to caves have been viewed as hazards and filled in, to prevent accidents or to keep out unwanted visitors. Both practices are destructive to the environment. Dumping of refuse leads to contamination of the underlying aquifer. A farmer near the Central Texas town of Boerne tells how his neighbor tossed the remains of a slain deer into a nearby sinkhole, only to be unpleasantly surprised later, when bits of fur began arriving with water from his well. For safety, bars can be placed across sinkhole entrances to caves without inhibiting aquifer recharge, but dumping of trash or bulldozing the entrance inhibits recharge and disrupts cave ecosystems, with dire consequences. For example, such action may destroy bat populations that hold local insects in check.

Caves for Recreation

Caves are increasingly a focus for recreation, and the number of cavers continues to grow. If you feel the pull of the "great indoors," be aware that this is not a hobby to begin on your own. Novices are advised to begin by touring a commercial cave to see how they like being underground. The next step is to join a group of experienced cavers.

The National Speleological Society (NSS) is a nonprofit organization founded in 1941 for the study and preservation of caves for scientific, scenic, and recreational purposes. The society's members have organized local chapters, commonly called *grottos*. Texas grottos are located in or near most major Texas cities. These groups offer training, sponsor trips, and generally welcome new members interested in caves and cave conservation. Members can help you get started with the proper equipment. For membership information and for the address of the grotto nearest you, contact NSS on Cave Avenue in Huntsville, Alabama 35810; tel. (205) 852–1300.

The Texas Speleological Association (TSA) is an independent regional society that works in close association with the NSS. It can be reached at 12102 Grimsley Drive, Austin, Texas 78759. TSA holds meetings, conventions, and caving projects throughout the year. Modest membership dues include a subscription to the *Texas Caver*, published six times a year and considered to be one of the country's finest caving publications.

References

Albright, Elaine. 1992. Where the bats are. *Texas Parks and Wildlife* 50 (no. 6): 48–50.

Bryan, Kelly. 1992. Into the night. *Texas Parks and Wildlife* 50 (no. 6): 40–45.

Matthews, William H., III. 1963. *The geologic story of Longhorn Cavern.* Guidebook 4. Austin: Bureau of Economic Geology, University of Texas at Austin. 50p.

National Speleological Survey. 1948. *The caves of Texas.* National Speleological Society Bulletin 10. Washington, D.C.: National Speleological Society. 136p.

Schmidly, David. 1991. *The bats of Texas.* College Station: Texas A&M Press. 188p.

Texas Water Commission. 1989. *Ground-water quality of Texas: an overview of natural and man-affected conditions.* Texas Water Commission Report 89–01. Austin: Texas Water Commission. 197p., 3 maps.

Veni, G. 1988. *The caves of Bexar County.* Speleological Monograph 2. Austin: Texas Memorial Museum. 300p.

Weisman, Dale. 1994. Splendors down under. *Texas Highways* 41 (no. 2): 4–11.

9 Texas and the Gulf of Mexico

The sea folds away from you like a mystery.
You can look at it and mystery never leaves it.
—Carl Sandburg, *Remembrance Rock*

Oceanography is an important aspect of earth science, and the Gulf of Mexico makes it an earth science topic pertinent to Texas. Our Gulf Coast has been called the "Texas Riviera." After all, it borders a mediterranean sea, just like the French and Italian rivieras. Oceanographers, you see, classify the Gulf of Mexico as a mediterranean sea (from the Latin *medius,* for middle, and *terra,* for land) because it is surrounded by a continental landmass with a relatively narrow opening to a much larger ocean. It is, of course, a minor sea, but one with an area of 615,000 square miles.

The Gulf of Mexico, then, is the world's ninth largest body of water and an important resource for both the United States and Texas. Gulf waters supply more than 50 percent of our nation's seafood, and its coastal wetlands serve as both nursery and refuge for many fish, shellfish, and fowl. Between 1956 and 1984, oil and gas development in the Gulf's Outer Continental Shelf generated federal revenue of more than $76 billion, second only to federal income tax. Of America's offshore oil and gas production, 90 percent comes from the Gulf of Mexico, and 40 percent of the total United States refining capacity is located along the Gulf. The Texas portion of the Gulf shore alone holds 65 percent of our nation's petrochemical capacity. Texas lays claim to 365 miles of Gulf shoreline (2,125 miles if you detour around the bays and lagoons). More than one-third of the state's population and economic activity is concentrated in that one-tenth of Texas that is within one hundred miles of the Gulf Coast.

Two professional geologic publications may tell you more than you want to know about the Gulf of Mexico. Salvador's *The Gulf of Mexico Basin* (1991) is a comprehensive summary of the geology of the Gulf and its shores. An atlas published by the National Oceanic and Atmospheric

FIG. 9.1. Mustang Island and Port Aransas, home of the Marine Science Institute, University of Texas at Austin, along the channel to the right. Courtesy *Texas Highways.*

Administration (1985) details the Gulf's bathymetry, temperatures, currents, and resources. Both are excellent sources, but a brochure published by the Marine Science Institute of the University of Texas at Austin (Amos and Amos 1987) provides a briefer introduction to the topic. Or, better yet, subscribe to *Texas Shores*, published quarterly at a modest rate by the Sea Grant College Program, Texas A&M University at Galveston, P.O. Box 1675, Galveston, Texas 77553.

Texas Oceanographic Institutions

The University of Texas at Austin and Texas A&M University are known as "flagship institutions" because they play leading roles in the state's educational and research efforts. In addition, both institutions actually have ships!

UT Marine Science Institute at Port Aransas

The Marine Science Institute of the University of Texas at Austin is located at Port Aransas, on the northeastern tip of Mustang Island (fig. 9.1).

Marine studies at the university had a rather stormy beginning. In the year 1900, the UT Board of Regents appropriated the magnificent sum of three hundred dollars to add a marine laboratory to the university's medical school at Galveston. In addition, Regent George W. Brackenridge donated a steam-powered launch to be used as a research vessel. Both the ship and the regents' plans were scuttled a few months later by the great Galveston hurricane. Fifteen years later, Regent Brackenridge came back with an offer of his 114-foot schooner, the *Navidad*, but misfortune persisted. Before the vessel went into service, it was badly damaged by a tropical storm and had to be sold.

So matters stood until 1940, when the mayor of Port Aransas offered the university a ten-acre tract at the northern tip of Mustang Island. The institute now occupies seventy-two acres there, with visitor center, museum, laboratories, library, classroom space, office, dormitory, and several vessels. The institute's flagship is the R.V. *Longhorn*, a steel-hulled trawler built in 1971 but beefed up in 1986 into a 105-foot research ship.

The institute's personnel conduct research and supervise master's and doctoral level students working on all aspects of oceanography. In addition, the institute operates its visitor center, holds teacher workshops, and annually hosts nearly ten thousand students of middle-school age or older. The high point of a typical class trip to the institute comes when students board the 57-foot trawler, *Katy*, and actually go to sea to collect and analyze water and sea-bed samples.

Texas A&M University and the Ocean Drilling Program

Texas A&M University offers master's and doctoral degrees in oceanography and operates the R.V. *Gyre*, a 182-foot research vessel based at Pelican Island, Galveston. In addition, the university manages what has to be considered the pearl of ocean-going research vessels, the JOIDES *Resolution* (fig. 9.2).

The Deep Sea Drilling Program (DSDP) was operated from 1968 to 1983 by the Scripps Institution of Oceanography in California, using the drillship *Glomar Challenger*. The DSDP achieved a brilliant record in confirming aspects of the plate tectonic theory such as sea-floor spreading and the relative youth and dynamic nature of the sea floor. DSDP became ODP (Ocean Drilling Program) in 1983, with a new drillship, the JOIDES *Resolution*, and a new institution, Texas A&M University, responsible for scientific operations.

The *Resolution* was named after the flagship used by Captain Cook on

FIG. 9.2. The JOIDES
Resolution at sea.
Courtesy Ocean Drilling Program,
Texas A&M University.

his second voyage of discovery to the Pacific Ocean, and JOIDES stands for Joint Oceanographic Institutions for Deep Earth Sampling. This drill-ship is one of the most modern ocean research vessels in the world. It is 471 feet long and 70 feet wide and has a displacement of 16,595 long tons. The ship's most distinctive feature sits on its deck: a derrick rising 202 feet above the waterline. Twelve computer-controlled propellers and a sophisticated satellite navigation system hold the ship on site as it drills in water depths of up to five miles and deploys almost six miles of drill string. The ship has twelve laboratories and carries a scientific crew of fifty and a ship's crew of sixty-five.

The ODP is an international consortium which includes ten major U.S. oceanographic institutions, including the Institute for Geophysics at the University of Texas. Texas A&M, however, is responsible for scientific operations. The university schedules the final scientific roster, plans the drilling schedule, and maintains the shipboard laboratories. After each cruise, it manages scientific meetings, distributes samples, edits and publishes scientific results, and acts as repository for some of the samples.

Origins of the Gulf of Mexico

The Gulf of Mexico is believed to have begun forming in Late Triassic time, as the supercontinent of Pangaea began the latest of its periodic breakups. In the Gulf area, great crustal blocks containing Africa, North America, and South America steadily moved away, while smaller fragments shifted and rotated less resolutely. One of these small crustal blocks—the one presently underlying Mexico's Yucatan Peninsula—is believed to have migrated southward, away from what is now Texas.

From Late Triassic until Middle Jurassic time, the Pangaean continental crust in the Gulf region was stretched and thinned until it broke into a series of great fault-bound valleys and mountains. These great rift basins became partly filled with sediment shed from adjacent mountains, and volcanic rock erupted through the thinned and broken crust. By Middle Jurassic time, parts of the Gulf region were below sea level. Salt began to be deposited across the Central Gulf as a result of the restricted circulation, shallow water, and warm climatic conditions of the time. Periodically, sea water also gained access to Gulf-margin basins, where it evaporated to lay down thick layers of salt.

As rifting continued into Late Jurassic time, a denser oceanic crust quickly formed in the central part of the Gulf during a relatively brief episode of sea-floor spreading. By Late Jurassic time, the major plate movements in the Gulf had ceased, the Yucatan block had completed its migration, and the Gulf of Mexico basin was firmly attached and moving with the North American plate. Vertical motion and sea-level changes, however, continued.

The Gulf basin has subsided substantially since Jurassic days, as the underlying crust has slowly cooled, contracted, and become more dense. A great thickness of sediment has been deposited in the Gulf, especially along its continental margins.

As the Gulf waters deepened and oceanic circulation became less restricted, salt deposition gave way to the widespread deposition of Jurassic and then Cretaceous limestone. Limestone was deposited all around the Gulf, and it continues to be deposited in Florida and the Yucatan. A Cretaceous episode of particularly high water flooded many continents, including North America. This left the thick limestone layer exposed from north of Dallas to Big Bend National Park.

As the Cretaceous period ended, the mighty Rocky Mountains began to form, and sediment-laden streams started flowing eastward toward the Gulf. The results are the broad, sandy Gulf Coastal Plain and today's coastal deltas, beaches, and barrier islands.

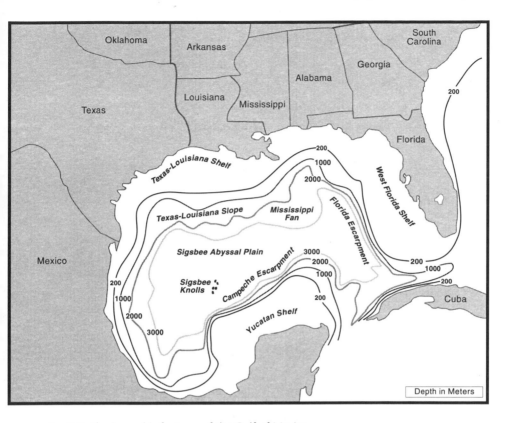

FIG. 9.3. Physiographic features of the Gulf of Mexico.
Map by Nancy Place; adapted from U.S. Department of Commerce, NOAA, Ocean Assessment Division (1985).

Physiographic Features of the Gulf

Figure 9.3 shows some of the topographic features of the Gulf of Mexico basin. About one-third of the Gulf is continental shelf—thick layers of sediment deposited on the submerged southern margin of the North American continent. The Texas Gulf Coastal Plain extends seaward to this broad continental shelf, which widens further toward Louisiana but narrows considerably south of Texas, off Mexico. The western Gulf shelf has numerous mounds formed by rising salt domes, as well as several canyons eroded during the Ice Age when the sea level was much lower.

The shelf passes Gulfward to a low-angle continental slope off Texas, contrasting markedly with the precipitous drops off Florida to the east and Yucatan to the south. A gigantic accumulation of sediment, the Mississippi delta and submarine fan, dominate the northern margin of the Gulf. The Central Gulf is occupied by the Sigsbee Abyssal Plain, one of the flattest places on earth, with an inclination of only three inches per nautical mile. The plain is broken only by the Sigsbee Knolls, the first place drilled by the DSDP and now known to be the sea-bottom expressions of rising salt domes. The deepest point in the Gulf is 12,700 feet below sea level, a level very close to the average depth of the world's oceans.

Currents and Tides

Warm Caribbean water flows past the Yucatan Peninsula and into the Gulf of Mexico, and then exits through the Florida Straits as the Gulf Stream (fig. 9.4). The Gulf part of this large system is known as the Loop Current because it makes a loop through the eastern Gulf before moving into the Atlantic. The Loop Current extends further into the Gulf during spring and less far during winter. A large, clockwise-rotating eddy or gyre is a fairly permanent feature in the western Gulf. Surface currents along the Texas coast vary with the seasons. They move northward during the summer but reverse in the winter to move southward, to the place where they converge with north-moving currents off Padre Island and are deflected offshore.

The tidal range in the Gulf, except during hurricanes and tropical storms, is a modest 1.5 feet. The Gulf Coast is somewhat unusual in that diurnal tides (one high and one low tide per day) predominate.

Salinity

Gulf water has an average salinity of 3.6 percent, slightly higher than average ocean values but normal for a mediterranean sea at this latitude. Much higher salinity can be found locally along sun-drenched Laguna Madre in South Texas and near the Texas-Louisiana border, where seeping brine has created a pocket of water with an extremely high salinity of about 20 percent.

Biology

Whales—including the sperm, pygmy sperm, dwarf sperm, pilot, killer, and pygmy killer whales—are known from the western Gulf. Ships may stir up schools of flying fish and attract dolphins to ride on water

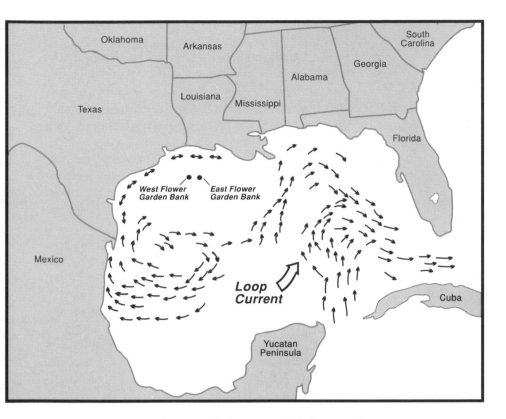

Fig. 9.4. Surface currents of the Gulf of Mexico and the location of the Flower Garden Banks. The double-tipped arrows along the Texas coast indicate that surface currents there tend to move southward in winter and northward in summer. Map by Nancy Place; adapted from U.S. Department of Commerce, NOAA, Ocean Assessment Division (1985).

pushed from the ships' bows. Occasionally, large whale sharks, manta rays, and the Portuguese man-of-war are seen. At night, schools of squid may appear. Deep-sea sport fishermen are attracted to the Gulf by blue and white marlin, sailfish, wahoo, and tuna. The fishing industry also harvests swordfish, tilefish, red snapper, and mackerel, to name just a few. Sharks are also harvested.

Sharks! Just the thought of swimming among them is enough to set your blood racing. But how likely is it that a shark actually might bite you? You are far more likely to win the Texas lottery. The Florida Museum of Natural History records shark attacks. Their records show that, from 1987 to 1992, Texas recorded an average of two shark attacks per year. About one in four shark attacks proves fatal, and the museum estimates that about fifteen people are killed worldwide by sharks each year. Crocodiles are a bigger danger, elephants kill ten times as many people, and bees kill fifty people for every one human who bumbles up against a shark.

Contact actually is much more frightening from the shark's point of view. More than a million sharks are killed for each human attacked by a shark. Sharks are killed for food, fun, and pharmaceuticals. Their jaws and teeth become trophies and jewelry, their skin is made into boots and purses, and their oil is an ingredient in many ointments, including a familiar product, Preparation H. On balance, then, Texas sharks give more than they get.

Perhaps the Gulf's most unusual biological feature is its Flower Garden. Located about 110 miles southeast of Galveston (fig. 9.4), the Flower Garden Banks National Marine Sanctuary is a unique ecosystem teetering at the ragged edge of its existence as the northernmost coral reefs on the North American continental shelf ("A Garden in the Gulf" 1991; Edwards 1994). Formed following sea-level rise at the end of the Ice Age, the reefs remained undisturbed for millennia, until their productivity attracted commercial fishermen. Turn-of-the-century snapper fishermen began recovering colorful plants and coral in their nets and started calling the area "the Flower Gardens."

The area contains two reefs, the East and West Flower Gardens, which have grown atop submarine bulges created by two of the Gulf's many rising salt domes. The East Flower Garden Bank is only 52 feet below sea level at its highest point, and it is capped by about four hundred acres of coral and algal reef. The West Flower Garden Bank, twelve miles westward, rises to within sixty-six feet of the surface; its reef covers approximately one hundred acres.

The reef environment supports a profusion of life forms, including some exotic ones (fig. 9.5). Already known from the reefs are 253 large invertebrate species, more than 175 species of fish, at least 80 species of algae, and 21 species of coral. Manta rays, loggerhead turtles, spotted dolphins, and 40-foot-long whale sharks also frequent the area.

Salt is not actually exposed on the sea bed, but its existence at depth has created an extremely unusual environment on the flank of the East

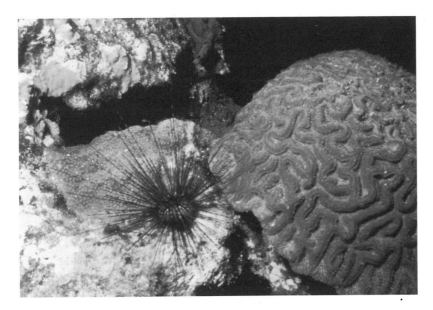

FIG. 9.5. Long-spined sea urchin browsing at night among star, brain, and fire corals in the Flower Garden Banks National Marine Sanctuary.
Photo by Stephen R. Gittings; courtesy Flower Garden Banks National Marine Sanctuary, U.S. National Oceanic and Atmospheric Administration.

Flower Garden Bank. There, 233 feet below the surface, dense seeping brine has created a thin saline pool, 80 feet in diameter and a scant 10 inches deep. Besides its extreme salinity; the brine pool contains dissolved hydrocarbon gases, no oxygen, and high levels of hydrogen sulfide—certainly conditions hostile to most marine life. Yet sulfide-oxidizing bacteria live along the thin interface between dense brine below and normal seawater above. At one end of this submarine "lake," brine spills down a submarine valley to mix with normal marine water. Here, specialized algae and bacteria thrive, attracting a community of hungry predators.

Although anchors, cables, and chains dragged by large ships have scarred the top of the reef, 19.2 square nautical miles at the East Bank and 22.5 square nautical miles at the West Bank now are under the protection of the National Marine Sanctuary Program administered by the U.S. National Oceanic and Atmospheric Administration. This means that anchoring vessels, mineral exploration, and fishing are regulated in these areas. Recreational dive boats and hook-and-line fishing boats still may use the area, but they must tie their lines to established mooring buoys anchored into long-dead coral rock.

Even though the Gulf is the ninth largest body of water in the world, it is feeling the impact of "civilization." One out of every six United States citizens lives in a state bordering the Gulf. Two-thirds of all the water draining from the U.S., pollution included, ends up in the Gulf of Mexico. Americans love the Gulf, but we have been loving it to death.

Recognizing this, the summer of 1992 through the summer of 1993 was designated by the United States Congress as the "Year of the Gulf." The idea was to focus national attention on a national treasure—to create the kind of commitment to saving the Gulf that has been given to restoring Chesapeake Bay and the Great Lakes.

Protecting such Gulf environments as the Flower Garden Banks benefits us all. The Flower Garden Banks are a reminder of the fragility of some of the ecosystems upon which we rely. We were well on the way to destroying that ecosystem before it was even understood. The recent discovery of those mysterious brine pools and the life forms they contain suggest that the Gulf of Mexico holds mysteries still. What other undiscovered secrets lie beneath Gulf waters?

References

Amos, A. F., and L. M. Amos, eds. 1987. "Window on the Sea." Port Aransas, Tex.: Marine Science Institute, University of Texas at Austin. 39p. Address: Port Aransas TX 78373-1267.

Edwards, Janet. 1994. Gardens beneath the sea. *Texas Highways* 41 (no 3): 4–9.

"A Garden in the Gulf." 1991. Poster TAMU-SG-92–102. College Station: Sea Grant Program, Texas A&M University. 1 sheet.

Salvador, A., ed. 1991. *The Gulf of Mexico Basin.* Volume J, *Geology of North America.* Boulder, Colo.: Geological Society of America. 568p.

U.S. Department of Commerce, National Oceanic and Atmospheric Administration, Ocean Assessment Division. 1985. *Gulf of Mexico coastal and ocean zones strategic assessment data atlas.* Washington D.C. 174p.

10 The Texas Environment

We do not inherit the Earth from our ancestors,
we borrow it for our children.
—Ralph Waldo Emerson

"Why is it," John Steinbeck asked, "that progress always looks like destruction?" In his day, environmental concerns were voiced by only a few voices crying in the wilderness. Today, with the wilderness gone and the problems facing us squarely, multitudes are enlisting in the environmental revolution. For the first time in the history of Western civilization, Earth is seen as a closed system—a kind of giant spaceship with limited fuel and supplies. To assure quality of life, perhaps even survival, Earth's environment must be protected. We are beginning to recognize the power humans possess to alter their environments; and, like Emerson, we are starting to appreciate that the effects of our mismanagement are cumulative and are likely to be passed on to successive generations.

Environmental problems come in all sizes. Some are global, others are specific to smaller areas. This chapter examines some home-grown varieties. Previous chapters have dealt with the possibilities of volcanic eruptions, damaging earthquakes, and even asteroid impacts. This chapter focuses on menaces of a more immediate nature, including problems of land, water, and air pollution.

Coastal Flooding and Erosion by Hurricanes

Flooding is probably the most widely experienced catastrophic natural hazard. Each year in the United States, flooding causes billions of dollars in damage. The sad truth is that the vast majority of floods are natural and, to some extent, predictable events. Texans are faced with two common flood problems: coastal flooding during hurricanes, and some of the most spectacular river flood events in the continental United States (table 10.1).

Imagine that you're approaching retirement. Before you "turn up your toes," you plan to let them spend a little time sifting through sand

Table 10.1 Notable Texas Floods

Date	Location	Deaths
1–5 Dec. 1913	Brazos River Basin	177
8–10 Sept. 1952	Pedernales and Guadalupe River Basins	52
6–28 June 1954	Lower Pecos River and Rio Grande	?
Apr.–May 1957	Pecos River to Sabine River	17
11 June 1965	Sanderson	26
28 Apr. 1966	Dallas County	14
11–12 May 1972	New Braunfels–Sequin Area	17
1–4 Aug. 1978	Edwards Plateau and North-Central Plains	33
24 May 1981	Austin	13
11–14 Oct. 1981	North-Central Texas	5
	($105 million damage)	
May 1990	North-Central and East Texas—Trinity and Red Rivers	12
	($1 billion damage)	
Oct. 1994	Southeast Texas—Lower Trinity and San Jacinto Rivers	19
	(10,000 people forced from homes)	

Source: *Texas Almanac,* 1992–93

on one of the many fine beaches between Sabine Pass and the Rio Grande. You invest in a barrier island condominium on a time-share plan. You may share the condo for ten years with snowbirds from Ohio, but one day the Gulf moves in to claim its previously unrecognized share of the partnership. Is this possible? Yes, say Paine and Morton (1989) of the Bureau of Economic Geology.

Moving eastward across the Gulf Coastal Plain, one encounters successively younger sedimentary rock formations, until arriving at the deltas, barrier islands, and lagoons of the Texas Gulf Coast. Obviously the general geologic trend has been a Gulfward migration of the coast, creating more of wonderful Texas. *Historic* coastal movement, however, has been quite another matter. While coastlines in specific areas may advance or retreat, surveys show that Texas lost about forty-one acres per year between 1974 and 1982 and as much as four hundred acres per year in the decade preceding that. These surveys suggest a long-established and continuing trend of beach retreat in Texas.

The agents affecting shoreline retreat are many. They include sea-level rise and land subsidence; coastal processes such as tides, currents, and waves; rainfall variations as they affect stabilizing vegetation; the influx of sediment from off- and on-shore sources; and human activities. The most rapid coastline changes, however, occur during hurricanes, when high water levels, wind, and waves combine to alter sections of the coast rapidly and drastically.

Records over the past one hundred years show that hurricanes have made landfall on the Texas coast at an average rate of about six per decade. Information on coastal erosion is available only for recent storms, however. In 1983, for example, Hurricane Alicia removed 54 million cubic feet of sand from the western two-thirds of Galveston Island—an average of 575 cubic feet per foot of shoreline. Alicia was a moderate hurricane (Saffir-Simpson rank of 3), with winds of 115 mph and a tidal surge of 8.5 feet above mean sea level. In 1980, Hurricane Allen, also packing winds of 115 mph, caused a spectacular shoreline retreat of 6 to 100 feet on Padre Island and cut thirty-eight channels across the island.

Barrier islands are particularly vulnerable to a hurricane's fury. Alicia, for example, caused an estimated $2 billion damage along the Texas coast (see chapter 3, figs. 3.10–3.13). The Galveston seawall, built to protect the city, is a monument to the hurricane that washed away two-thirds of the city's buildings and at least six thousand of the region's citizens.

Alicia and Allen were moderate hurricanes, and the Galveston hurricane occurred nearly a century ago. Carla was the last really large hurricane to strike the Texas coast, and the vast majority of current coastal residents never have experienced a hurricane like Carla. The storm, in September, 1961, covered the entire Gulf of Mexico as it approached. Winds in excess of 75 mph were recorded almost all along the Texas coast, and velocities near the storm center were estimated at over 175 mph. When the next hurricane like Carla comes, the seawalls, modern weather forecasting, and evacuation plans likely will keep fatalities to a low level, but property damage will be enormous.

River Flooding

River systems are an important and treasured part of the natural landscape. They provide recreation, are an economic resource, and supply arid areas of Texas with much-needed water—occasionally too much water. For the river, it's business as usual: carving the landscape; conveying water and sediment down a gradient to the ocean; providing the raw material for deltas, beaches, barrier islands, and even future coal fields, petroleum reservoirs, and mountain ranges. The river channel and flood plains are part of the river's domain. Unfortunately, humans have a tendency to build on these flat areas near rivers, and we only realize that we are trespassing when disaster strikes. Even then, in a courageous display of frontier grit, many valiantly pick up the pieces, put their lives back in order, and, shouting "Viva Indianola," rebuild. In the past, government-supported flood-insurance programs helped sustain this cycle of ignorance and pain.

Hydrogeologists divide river flooding into two types, upstream floods and downstream floods. Downstream floods occur when a large weather system dumps an enormous volume of rain over a wide area. Although the upstream part of the drainage system may be able to handle the water, the many swollen tributaries overwhelm the downstream part of the system. Downstream floods are characterized by slowly rising water which persists for days or weeks, as in the 1990 flooding along the Trinity and Red rivers in Northeast Texas, or the 1993 flooding in the upper Mississippi River Valley.

Upstream floods, more sudden and spectacular, are commonly known as flash floods. They occur when intense local rainfall swamps the upstream part of the drainage system. Upstream floods may dissipate downstream as the river's capacity to carry water increases. Flash floods are common in hilly or mountainous terrain that is subjected to periodic torrential rains, especially if the region is arid or semi-arid so that vegetation is sparse and the soil is thin. These conditions are more than met in the Texas Hill Country and in Trans-Pecos Texas.

Trans-Pecos Texas: Sanderson

Suppose that, water-shy by now, you decide to retire west of the Pecos, perhaps in Sanderson. Here are directions: follow U.S. Highway 90 west until the live oaks begin to resemble broccoli sprouts, cross the Pecos River near Langtry, go past Pumpville and Dryden, and stop just this side of Hell's Half Acre. Sound arid enough?

Sanderson, in the southeastern corner of Trans-Pecos Texas, is a quiet town in a narrow canyon on the floodplain of Sanderson Creek. Upstream, at the western edge of town, Sanderson Creek is joined by Three-Mile Draw. On June 11, 1965, following rains of up to eight inches in just two hours, a flash flood spilling out of Three-Mile Draw overwhelmed Sanderson Creek and occupied the floodplain. Twenty-six persons drowned, and 450 were left homeless. The powerful surge even uncovered graves in the local cemetery and swept headstones as far as four miles downstream.

Today, a series of dams upstream from Sanderson are designed to intercept runoff and protect the town. It has been said, however, that earthen dams can break with consequences even more disastrous than if nature had been allowed to take its course.

Central Texas Flooding

Perhaps you decide on a little cabin on the Pedernales River in the Texas Hill Country near Luckenbach, Texas, "with Willie, Waylon, and the Boys." Before you move to LBJ country, however, you should be aware of some special hazards associated with Central Texas drainage systems.

Probably no place in the United States is more prone to flash floods than Central Texas. Folks there say things like "I'll be there if the good Lord's willin' and the creeks don't rise" and mean it. Geologic, topographic, and biological factors conspire in Central Texas to produce flash flooding of gargantuan proportions (Baker 1975). First, the Balcones Escarpment forms a topographic barrier trending perpendicular to moisture-laden air moving in from the Gulf. Gulf-derived air is deflected upward as it encounters the escarpment. This process can feed moisture into convective thunderstorms that tend to linger above the same location, producing huge accumulations of local rainfall. When large tropical storms are involved, the results can be astonishing. Mean annual precipitation along the Balcones Escarpment ranges from about 30 inches near Austin to about 20 inches at Del Rio, yet that amount can be dumped in a single day.

In September, 1921, for example, Thrall, northeast of Austin, received 38.2 inches of rain in one 24-hour period. At least as spectacular was the May 31, 1935, cloudburst at D'Hanis, between San Antonio and Uvalde, that produced 22 inches of rainfall in two hours and forty-five minutes! Only in Texas can you get your yearly annual average precipitation in less time than it takes to play a football game.

The thin soils, sparse vegetation, impermeable bedrock, and narrow canyons of Central Texas promote run-off rates that make the flooding associated with these storms as sudden and spectacular as the storms themselves. In September, 1952, for example, a tropical storm generated

FIG. 10.1. Flooding on the Guadalupe River at Kerrville in summer, 1978. Courtesy *Texas Highways*.

from 20 to 26 inches of rainfall in the Pedernales drainage area (including Luckenbach), producing a flood crest of 48 feet at the Johnson City bridge. The flood probably would have been maintained through to Austin, had not Mansfield Dam stopped its advance. Flood crests of 40 to 50 feet are not uncommon in Central Texas, and depths of up to 60 feet have been recorded in narrow sections of Central Texas river systems like those of the Guadalupe, Colorado, and Pedernales rivers.

The Guadalupe River rises from its spring-fed north and south forks in western Kerr County and flows eastward through the beautiful Texas Hill Country. During the first week in August, 1978, tropical storm Amelia dumped more than 20 inches of rain on the headwaters of the Medina, Sabinal, and Guadalupe rivers (figs. 10.1 and 10.2). The Manatt Ranch, 11 miles northwest of Medina, received more than 48 inches of rain in 52 hours, establishing a new U.S. record for rainfall in a 72-hour period (Schroder et al. 1987). The Guadalupe River at Kerrville rose at the astonishing rate of a foot per minute. Downstream at Spring Branch, at the U.S. Highway 281 bridge, the river reached a level 59 feet above

FIG. 10.2. Flood debris left by the Medina River at Bandera in summer, 1978. Courtesy *Texas Highways*.

normal. In just one day, 149 billion muddy gallons poured down the Guadalupe River and raced on toward the Balcones Escarpment, whose cities had been battered by past floods.

Cities founded on rivers draining the Edwards Plateau occasionally are victimized by the water their founding fathers so eagerly sought. In April, 1900, for example, Austin's 68-foot-high McDonal Dam crumbled before a Colorado River flood, releasing a wall of water that drowned twenty-three persons and injured two hundred others. Shoal Creek, a tributary to the Colorado River in Austin, has a recent history of flooding problems, undoubtedly exacerbated by the urban development of its drainage basin. During the night of May 24–25, 1981, 10 inches of rain sent the lower part of Shoal Creek over its banks and into part of Austin. Thirteen people drowned, and the flooding caused damage worth about $40 million.

New Braunfels experienced a similar fate in 1972. New Braunfels is located where the spring-fed Comal River meets the Guadalupe River as it leaves the Texas Hill Country. The Guadalupe River upstream from

New Braunfels drains 1,518 square miles. The city is protected from drainage in most of that basin by Canyon Dam, ten miles to the north. Only 86 square miles of arroyo-covered Hill Country lie between Canyon Dam and New Braunfels—surely too little to worry about, right?

On the evening of May 11, 1972, a series of intense thunderstorms formed southwest of New Braunfels and moved northeastward along the Balcones Escarpment. The storm lasted only four hours but dropped up to 16 inches of rain, most of it in just one hour. The storm precipitated, so to speak, a classic upstream flood. The Guadalupe River rose 28 feet in only two hours, claimed seventeen victims, and caused property damage valued at $17.5 million.

Unstable Rock Formations and Soils

Inconceivable as it sounds, some Texans have to live (if that's the right word) with the possibility that their world quite literally may crumble and fall. The problem has to do with surface stability, which in Texas ranges from clay-rich soils that shrink and swell to the catastrophic collapse of the surface in the form of sinkholes and landslides.

Some sedimentary rock formations, although millions of years old, consist of loose sand or soft clay which can be quite unstable. Certain clay beds have the very undesirable engineering characteristic of behaving like a plastic or even a liquid if their water content is high enough. The Del Rio Clay, a fossil-rich Cretaceous-age marl that is widespread in Central Texas, is notorious for slope failure problems. It is an unstable rock unit to be avoided by builders, but it is not as great a problem as expansive soils.

Expansive soils may not seem as threatening as floods, volcanoes, hurricanes, or earthquakes. Humans rarely if ever lose their lives to slowly widening quarter-inch cracks. Nevertheless, in the U.S., the annual cost of expansive soils is billions of dollars—greater than any other single hazardous natural process. Expansive soils can develop over limestone containing even a small amount of clay. As the limestone dissolves, the insoluble clay ends up as those alternately sticky (when wet) and brick-hard (when dry) soils that cover parts of the state. Clay comes in a number of types, and montmorillonite is a common clay associated with expansive soil. Montmorillonite expands by as much as 1,500 percent when water is available. Fortunately, soils tend to contain many constituents besides clay, but soil expansion and contraction of even 3 percent can be hazardous to structures. The problem, as you might imagine, is most severe in regions having distinctive wet and dry seasons; and Central Texas, with its limestone bedrock, dry summers, and wet springs, has abundant expansive soil.

Surface Subsidence along the Texas Gulf Coast

Surface subsidence (sinking) is a major environmental problem along the Gulf Coast, where ground water, oil, and gas have been extracted from the porous sandy layers of sand-clay sequences (Brown et al. 1974). The removal of fluids from the sands causes a pressure drop that facilitates the expulsion of water from interlayered beds of clay. The resulting compaction can be quite noticeable at the surface, particularly if that surface originally was just above sea level. The National Geodetic Survey periodically determines the altitude of a line of bench markers along the Gulf Coast. Although measurements taken from 1906 to 1982 show an average surface subsidence of less than 0.5 feet, the problem is much more severe in the rice irrigation area of Jackson and Matagorda counties and in the populous Houston-Galveston area.

The entire Houston-Galveston area sits on a giant wedge of mud and sand that is slowly compacting. The area around the San Jacinto Monument, for example, subsided six feet between 1900 and 1964. In the Pasadena–Houston Ship Channel vicinity, where low-lying areas now are experiencing increased flooding during storms (fig. 10.3), as much as nine feet of subsidence has occurred in that period. Houston is fifty-five feet above sea level, an elevation Houstonians can live with, but Houston has not escaped compaction problems. Not all of the sediment beneath Houston is compacting at the same rate, and differential compaction causes breaks known as growth faults. Although earthquakes are not associated with growth faults, their slow, inexorable movement damages homes and other overlying structures. Geologists think that the problem will abate as the underlying petroleum becomes depleted and Houstonians switch to surface water sources like the lakes Livingstone and Houston.

Sinkholes in Limestone Formations

Less of a problem but far more spectacular than slow surface subsidence is the wholesale collapse of a small area to form a sinkhole. Sinkholes usually are associated with limestone caves, and the process by which they are formed is fairly well understood. As a cave grows, its roof receives less and less support. Eventually it may collapse to form a sinkhole. Caves are enlarged by solution during times of high water, but

FIG. 10.3. Subsidence-induced flooding at the Brownwood Subdivision of Baytown, Texas. Land there is now nine feet lower than it was in the 1940s. Although raised eight feet over the years, this home has had to be abandoned. Courtesy U.S. National Oceanic and Atmospheric Administration.

sinkholes tend to form during droughts, when the cave roof is deprived of the cave water's buoyant support. Several sinks, including the spectacular Winter Park sink, developed during the Florida drought of 1981. Amazed onlookers watched as a monster hole grew to be about a block in size and swallowed trees, a house, two businesses, several automobiles, and part of a community swimming pool. The number of sinkholes formed in prehistoric times across the Edwards Plateau probably numbers in the thousands, and it is only a matter of time until the next one forms.

Sinkholes Associated with Salt

Two sets of circumstances—the salt water basins and arid climate prevalent during the assembly of the continent Pangaea late in the Paleozoic era; and the Mesozoic opening of the Gulf of Mexico—left beds of salt below parts of West Texas and large regions of the Texas Gulf Coast. These events made Texas both a leader among states supplying salt and a likely site for a high-level nuclear waste dump (discussed later). They also created a salt problem that Texas can't seem to lick.

The Texas Bureau of Economic Geology has investigated salt beds and domes for their economic value and as possible disposal sites for hazardous waste. Their research has documented a surprising number of natural subsidence features over near-surface salt domes, as well as subsidence structures induced by the production of the sulfur, oil, gas, and brine associated with salt. Salt-related sinkholes usually consist of shallow sag-depressions formed by gradual subsidence, but steep-walled collapse structures do occasionally develop catastrophically (Mullican 1988).

Gulf Coast Salt Domes

Deep-lying salt is lighter than the surrounding rock; and, although solid, it may rise in a magma-like fashion. In the arid climate of southern Iran, salt has risen to the surface in forms that mimic volcanoes and lava flows. Along the Texas Gulf Coastal Plain, the locations of some shallow salt domes are marked by mild uplifts, while others exhibit topographic depressions occupied by small lakes. These depressions form as a result of natural subsidence and collapse occurring when salt domes rise into zones of fresh, or saline but unsaturated, ground water. The dissolution of the salt deprives the overlying material of support and causes it slowly to sag or violently to collapse into the underlying void.

Natural subsidence above salt domes may be drastically accelerated by the extraction of salt, petroleum, gas, or sulfur. Subsidence, occasionally sudden and catastrophic, has been documented for the ten most productive of the fourteen sulfur-producing domes in the Houston area. Boling Dome, southeast of Houston, has produced almost eighty million long tons of sulfur, to become the largest producer of sulfur in the United States; it has a larger volume of man-induced subsidence than any other dome in Texas (exceeding 42 feet in depth and affecting 2.2 square miles).

Some of the sinkholes formed suddenly. In 1983, for example, a hole 25 feet deep and 250 feet in diameter formed along F.M. Road 442, directly over the crest of Boling Dome (fig. 10.4).

Collapse associated with deep mines can take years to reach the surface. Orchard Dome, for example, 17 miles north of Boling Dome, produced sulfur from as deep as 3,156 feet below the surface, the deepest Frasch mining operation in the world. Sulfur production started in 1924, but the first sinkhole did not appear until 1941. By 1985, twenty-two sinkholes had formed.

FIG. 10.4. This sinkhole formed suddenly on August 12, 1983, over Boling
Dome near Houston. Courtesy *Texas Highways.*

In addition to sulfur, thirteen Texas domes have been mined for salt,
either by underground methods or by using brine wells. The Palestine
Salt and Coal Company mined salt from the Palestine Dome in East
Texas by drilling wells into the salt, injecting fresh water, and then
removing the brine with compressed air. It took time, but sinkholes
eventually formed at every old brine well. One sinkhole formed in 1978,
at least forty-one years after mining ceased.

A bizarre incident involving an underground salt mine and a surface
drilling operation at Louisiana's Jefferson Island Dome, although not in
Texas, illustrates another potential hazard (Autin 1984). The surface
above Jefferson Island Dome was the site of a subsidence feature occupied by Lake Peigneur. On November 20, 1980, a Texaco well being
drilled along the southern flank of the dome penetrated the underground salt mine and created a connection between the lake bottom
and the mine. During the next four hours, the drilling rig, a supply
barge, and Lake Peigneur all were sucked into the Jefferson Island salt
mine.

The Jefferson situation was unusual, but subsidence at salt domes has been associated with drilling operations and with the removal of oil and gas in Texas, too. One example, occurring on October 9, 1929, was observed by two men who reported the sudden formation of a seventy- to ninety-foot hole above the Sour Lake oil field at Sour Lake Salt Dome in Hardin County.

Salt Beds of the Panhandle Region

Thick sequences of soluble late Paleozoic (Permian) salt and gypsum underlie parts of the Texas Panhandle. The dissolution of underlying salt and gypsum seems to be a major factor in the development of the *playas* characteristic of the local landscape. The process and its effect on manmade structures is the subject of a report by Simpkins et al. (1981), who documented over four hundred sinkholes and collapse depressions in Hall County alone. The sinkholes generally are circular to oval in shape and range from a few feet to 330 feet in diameter. Sinkhole formation is a remarkably active process, a fact demonstrated by the formation of thirty-six sinkholes between 1940 and 1979 in a study area of just 120 square miles. Although the population density in this region is low, the process has caused structural damage to highways and dams and has caused reservoirs and stock tanks to lose water to underlying fractures.

A spectacular example of sinkhole formation occurred in 1980, just southwest of the Panhandle near the town of Wink (Baumgardner, Hoadley, and Goldstein 1982). Dubbed the Wink Sink, the collapse was first noticed on June 3. By June 9, the sink was 360 feet in diameter and 110 feet deep (fig. 10.5). Natural dissolution of the underlying salt beds—enhanced, perhaps, by the presence of a fifty-two-year-old abandoned well—is believed to have been the cause.

Salt beds have been used as sources for salt, brine, sulfur, oil, and natural gas. Spindletop salt dome, near Beaumont, was the world's first major oil field, and exploited salt domes in Texas and Louisiana now serve as storage sites for the millions of barrels of crude oil in the Strategic Petroleum Reserve. As if they haven't contributed enough, salt beds were, until recently, considered potential sites for nuclear waste. Research by the Texas Bureau of Economic Geology, however, has shown salt beds and domes to be unsuitable for long-term storage of hazardous waste. They are dynamic environments, prone to mild subsidence and wild collapse.

FIG. 10.5. Wink Sink, Winkler County, Texas, as it appeared on June 5, 1980. The water surface is about thirty-three feet below the rim.
Courtesy Robert J. Baumgardner, Jr.

Crazy Cat Mountain

At first glance, Crazy Cat Mountain appears to be nothing more than an imaginatively named hill tucked against the steep western slope of the Franklin Mountains, just uphill from the tranquil campus of the University of Texas at El Paso (fig. 10.6). It wasn't quiet when Crazy Cat formed, however. The hill is a conglomeration of rock fragments created when great slabs of limestone strata broke loose from the mountains above and crashed to the valley floor. Erosion, it seems, is undercutting the steeply inclined rock layers of the Franklin Mountains and setting the stage for disaster. Perhaps the slide was triggered by an earthquake or by some unusually heavy rains. The landslide is clearly of ancient origin, but it is clear too that younger brother and sister slabs, tilted and undercut, sit atop the crest of the Franklin Mountains, awaiting their turns at the slide.

It is very human to feel that natural disasters are some sort of aberration, that nature should, somehow, be made to submit to our will. We use the

FIG. 10.6. The Franklin Mountains, with Crazy Cat Mountain in the foreground to the left of center. Photo by author.

term *natural disaster*, but, when we fail to understand that property will always be damaged and lives lost to nature's fury, we act as if disasters were unnatural. Some disasters are natural, and there is little or nothing we can do to control or prevent them. But science provides insight into nature, and knowledge is power. Understanding nature affords us the opportunity to get out of nature's way when and where we deem it prudent. We can avoid or minimize the damage to property and the loss of life that nature can inflict.

Ground Water Contamination

Contaminated water, a problem of ever-increasing proportions, has many causes. This chapter explores some of the major sources of water contamination in Texas.

At the outset, however, two words of caution are in order. First, as my old chemistry professor said, "Poison is poison in poisonous doses; eat enough potatoes and it will kill ya." His point was that you can't label a substance as toxic without specifying at what concentration it is toxic.

Table 10.2   Dissolved Mineral Constituents in the Water:
Their Sources and Significance

Silica	Common rock and soil constituent that can form scale in pipes
Iron	Common rock constituent which oxidizes in air form a reddish stain. Large amounts cause an unpleasant taste.
Calcium and Magnesium	Dissolved especially from limestone, dolomite, and gypsum. Cause most hard water problems, deposit scale, increase soap consumption
Sodium and Potassium	Naturally found in rocks and in large amounts in oil-field brine and sea water. High concentration as a chloride gives a salty taste, and high sodium limits water used for agriculture.
Bicarbonate and Carbonate	From the action of carbon dioxide in water on limestone and dolomite. Cause hard water when combined with calcium and magnesium. Causes formation of scale in pipes and boilers.
Sulfate	Dissolved from gypsum and iron sulfides. Can cause a bitter taste and act as a laxative.
Chloride	Dissolved from rocks, large amounts in oil-field brine, sea water, and some industrial effluent. Gives a salty taste in combination with sodium, increases corrosiveness of water.
Fluoride	Dissolved in small quantities from rocks, reduces the incidence of tooth decay; but in higher concentrations may cause mottling of teeth.
Nitrate	Decaying organic matter, sewage, fertilizer, barnyard or feed lot runoff. May give water a bitter taste and encourage algal growth.

Source: Texas Water Commission (1989).

For example, is zinc toxic? Diseases in plants and animals have been related to both excesses and deficiencies in zinc. Contaminants are a problem only when they are at certain levels.

Second, while any water contamination is undesirable, not all of it is unnatural. Natural as well as artificial processes produce higher than desirable concentrations of a variety of substances. Table 10.2 shows some dissolved mineral constituents commonly found in water, their major sources, and some typical consequences of excessive amounts.

An excellent overview of water quality problems is *Ground-Water Quality of Texas: An Overview of Natural and Man-Affected Conditions* (Texas Water Commission 1989), the major source for the following information. (Note: The Texas Water Commission now is called the Texas Natural Resource Conservation Commission, or TNRCC.) Sources of contamination covered by the report include waste disposal sites, disposal of sewage, mining and agricultural activities, accidental spills, and intentional dumping.

Buried waste can be a significant source of contamination if water is able to pass through it, leach contaminants, and transport them to an aquifer. The composition of the contaminated fluid, termed *leachate*, depends upon the waste at the disposal site. These range from large industrial wastes to leaking graveyard coffins.

Industrial Waste

Texas is the nation's largest producer of hazardous waste. The TNRCC estimates that we generate 37 million metric tons per year, 17 percent of the U.S. total and more than twice as much as any other state. The TNRCC divides waste into three classes, according to its hazard potential.

Class I waste poses a substantial danger to human health or the environment when improperly managed. Class I wastes include solids that are flammable, corrosive, strongly irritating, or capable of generating sudden pressure or heat during decomposition.

The hazard potential of Class II waste is relatively low. They are generally degradable, present a relatively low level of toxicity, and become a significant problem only in large quantities. Among Class II solids are such common things as paper, wood, grease, and plant trash.

Class III wastes are inert and essentially insoluble objects such as rock, glass, dirt, and certain plastics.

The most common system for disposing of industrial wastes is the landfill. In 1980, Texas had 376 registered, on-site industrial landfills, 213 of which received Class I wastes. Most of these are located along the Texas Gulf Coast, especially in the Houston and Beaumont areas. Nationwide, as of August, 1987, there were 808 abandoned waste sites listed on the EPA's national priority list. Commonly called "Superfund Sites," they are eligible for federally funded cleanup. Texas has twenty-two of these. Again, most lie in the "Golden Triangle." Less dangerous sites may not make the national priority list, but they still pose a problem, and Texas has developed a registry of its own. As of September, 1991, Texas listed

38 sites on its proposed state Superfund registry. Of these sites, 7, including 4 of the 10 highest priority locations, are in Harris County.

Municipal Landfills

The sanitary landfill is the standard and preferred method for disposing of municipal solid wastes. Landfills are located and engineered to minimize environmental hazards, but they probably never work perfectly. Major problems occur when there are inadequate controls on the generation and migration of leachate. In the past, little thought was given to dump sites, and older landfills usually were left unlined and often uncovered. According to the Texas Department of Health, as of 1984, there were 950 active and several hundred closed and abandoned municipal solid waste sites known to exist in Texas. Landfills are believed to be a significant threat to ground water. A 1988 EPA investigation, for example, confirmed local ground water contamination near landfill sites in the Dallas–Fort Worth, San Antonio, and Houston areas.

Graveyards

Old graveyards, where wooden coffins and nonleakproof caskets are common, are considered to be a potential, if not a great, source of ground-water contamination. There are, of course, hundreds of cemeteries in Texas. The Bastrop County map shows about 120 in that county alone, and Texas probably has more graveyards than any other state. Certainly ground-water conditions should be among the criteria considered during selection of a cemetery site, and a hydrogeologists should be consulted when locating a water well near an old cemetery.

Industrial Waste Disposal Wells

Texas has a large petrochemical industry, expertise in well technology, and available reservoir rock at depth. It is not surprising, then, that Texas, of all the states, leads in the use of injection wells for the disposal of industrial waste. More than half the state's industrial waste—over five billion gallons each year—is flushed into subsurface reservoirs. Fluids injected range from practically pure rain water, through sewage effluent, to highly toxic chemical and radioactive substances. In general, the wells inject waste into highly saline zones well below, and isolated from, potable water-bearing horizons. While the potential for ground water contamination is obvious, if properly engineered, the waste is contained and isolated from the near-surface environment, and it could probably even be recovered if the need arose.

Sewage Disposal Systems

Most Texas households are serviced by municipal sewage lines, and leakage from these systems, particularly older systems, can be a problem. Most rural and small-town Texans utilize on-site disposal systems. In recent years, the septic tank with subsurface drain field has become the rural Texas standard. As recently as 1980, however, it was estimated that over 120,000 Texans relied on that old standby, the house behind the house, to meet their needs. Under adverse conditions, untreated sewage can escape the soil zone and pass to the local aquifer. The dangers of untreated sewage range from pathogenic bacteria to a safe but annoying deterioration in taste. The Texas Department of Health estimated that in 1985 there were about 1,212,600 septic tanks in operation in the state. Because each tank probably impacts the ground water to some degree, there is cause for concern, especially in highly populated areas located over unfavorable geologic settings.

Abandoned Wells

It is ironic, but water wells are considered to be one of the greatest sources of ground-water pollution. The problem involves improperly constructed and improperly abandoned wells. Many people remember an incident that occurred in October, 1987, when eighteen-month-old Jessica McClure of Midland fell into an eight-inch open well and was trapped twenty-two feet below ground for fifty-eight agonizing hours before being rescued. The heart-rending story illustrates one of the hazards associated with improperly abandoned wells.

Uncapped wells also allow surface contaminants to enter the water supply, and improperly constructed wells may connect between water horizons of unequal quality. The Texas Water Development Board estimates that Texas has some 600,000 water wells, with 20,000 additional wells being drilled annually. There may be as many as 150,000 abandoned wells. Because the vast majority of these are probably improperly abandoned, the dimensions of the problem are great.

Leaking Underground Storage Tanks

You may be surprised to hear that the Texas Water Development Board considers LUST to be one of the major sources of ground water pollution. This LUST, however, is an acronym for Leaking Underground Storage Tanks. It is estimated that over 150,000 underground tanks exist in Texas and that about 38,500 of them will eventually become LUST. As of July 12, 1988, there were about 1,000 confirmed "leakers," with an average of 62 being added to that number each month.

Petroleum and Chemical Spills

Texas has 250,000 miles of highways, 12,753 miles of railroads, and 202,623 miles of hydrocarbon pipelines (72,615 for oil and 130,008 of natural gas). Accidental spills of hazardous substances transported by truck, rail, and pipeline are becoming a common occurrence. In addition to accidental spills, illegal or "midnight dumping" is an all-too-common occurrence (one might even say practice) that must be stopped. The TNRCC reported 1,592 dumping incidents in 1987, but the problem appears to be highly localized. Nearly half of the reported dumpings took place in just four counties (Harris, 281; Jefferson, 209; Tarrant, 123; Dallas, 116), while many rural counties had no reported incidents at all.

Petroleum Industry

It is estimated that in Texas over 1.5 million holes have been drilled in search of hydrocarbons. Opportunities exist for pollution of surface and ground water while drilling, during production, and after abandonment if the well is improperly capped. Oil-field brine is an especially great problem. Over time, oil wells unfortunately tend to produce less petroleum and more oil-field brine. Ultimately, wells cease to be profitable and must be capped. In the early days of the petroleum industry, brine was discharged into the nearest ravine or stream. Later, evaporation pits lined with an impermeable layer became the standard. Starting in 1969, nearly all brine had to be piped or hauled to injection wells for disposal. Some "midnight dumpers" never make it to their legal destinations.

In earlier days, wells were abandoned to became conduits for aquifer contamination. Today, all aspects of the industry require permits and are subject to regulation. Still, accidents occur, and careless or unscrupulous individuals continue to cause significant amounts of environmental damage.

Mining

Surface mining is less dangerous and less expensive than underground methods, so mining is done by surface methods whenever possible. Surface mining, of course, directly impacts the land, causing noise, dust, and polluted runoff water. More than two hundred thousand acres of Texas land is disrupted by mining. The largest contributor is the sand, gravel, and crushed rock industry, but several large coal strip mines pose special problems. Once exposed, constituents in coal react with the atmosphere and water to produce acid and release heavy metals. To mitigate the problem, water is removed from the mine site before the coal is mined, and the mining site is returned to its natural state following extraction of the coal.

Farming and Ranching

When cattle roamed the range, the range might have gotten a little messy, but only in spots. Today these critters are crowded, well, like cattle into feed lots. Each year, some four to five million of our bovine buddies check into one these "fat farms" (there are over two hundred such feed lots in Texas) for four or five months of good living. During this stay, each produces about a thousand pounds of waste that is rich in nitrogen, phosphates, chlorides, bacteria, and viruses. Without proper controls, the local environment can be overwhelmed. Similar problems are posed by hog, poultry, sheep, and dairy operations.

Intensive agriculture also has its environmental costs. Each year Texas farmers use several million tons of fertilizer to increase the productivity of the soil. Plants simply can't use every bit of the phosphorus, nitrogen, and potassium thrown at them. The unused phosphorus may be transported away to contribute to eutrophication of streams and lakes. Nitrogen can be oxidized to a polluting gas or to nitrate, a common ground-water pollutant.

Pesticides are an additional problem (fig. 10.7). The EPA estimates that there are more than fifty thousand licensed pesticide products, together containing some 1,200 to 1,400 different active ingredients. Texas, with thirty million acres of cropland, accounts for an estimated 10 percent of all pesticides used in this country, and the TNRCC believes that pesticide use can contaminate ground water. In 1984, for example, 34 of the 101 wells tested in Howard and Martin counties contained arsenic (formerly used in pesticides) in concentrations that exceeded federal safe drinking-water standards.

Air Pollution Problems

"Air," someone once said, "is of no great importance until you're not getting any." For years Texans have taken clean air for granted or

Fɪɢ. 10.7. A crop duster applies pesticides to a Panhandle cotton field. Courtesy *Texas Highways.*

joked that you shouldn't trust any air you can't see. The Texas Air Control Board (now part of the TNRCC) was established in 1965 to safeguard the air we breath. The board's regulatory powers come from the Federal Clean Air Act and the Texas Clean Air Act. It is headquartered in Austin, with regional offices in Abilene, Beaumont, Corpus Christi, El Paso, Fort Worth, Harlingen, Houston, Lubbock, Odessa, San Antonio, Tyler, and Waco. The TNRCC operates about thirty air monitoring sites, conducts research, issues permits, and investigates some five thousand citizen complaints per year.

Acid Rain

The Texas Air Control Board began monitoring Texas rain in 1979 and has found that, while acid rain occurs throughout Texas on a routine basis, the problem is much less severe than in the industrial northeastern United States. Acid rain occurs most frequently and with greatest acidity in East Texas, especially near lignite and coal power plants.

Ozone

Ozone is created by solar radiation on atmospheric gases. Stratospheric ozone forms a protective barrier against harmful ultraviolet radiation, but ozone in the lower atmosphere causes lung damage, harms vegetation, and deteriorates such products as rubber, plastics, nylon, and paint. Ozone is a problem mainly in the daytime, in the summer, near major cities where hydrocarbons are burned in large amounts. Ozone forms as smog drifts with the prevailing wind, and the most polluted areas may not be downtown areas. The prevailing summer wind is from the Gulf, so ozone levels typically are highest on the northwestern sides of major cities. Federal law allows ozone levels of less than 0.12 parts per million when averaged over an hour. If a city exceeds that level three times in three consecutive years, it becomes a "designated nonattainment area." Folks in designated nonattainment areas must comply with certain restrictions on the use of fuels and other volatile organic compounds. Texas ozone nonattainment areas include the Beaumont–Port Arthur, Dallas–Fort Worth, El Paso, and Houston-Galveston areas. The good news for Texas is that the average number of high ozone days has decreased over the last decade. The bad news is that many Texans still are exposed to ozone levels above the federally established health standard, and ozone continues to be the state's most pressing air pollution problem.

Decreasing Visibility

In addition to ozone and acid rain, the TNRCC monitors carbon monoxide, sulfur dioxide, nitrogen dioxide, fine suspended particulate matter, lead, and haze. Compared with the rest of the United States, Texas does fairly well in these areas, but there are trouble spots. For example, the TNRCC considers the decline in visibility in the Dallas area to be the most striking illustration of deterioration in air quality in Texas in the past twenty years. Two types of visible pollution have been identified in Dallas: an early morning brown cloud caused mainly by vehicle exhaust and wood burning, and a widespread, persistent white haze that appears to be the result of sulfates from coal and lignite combustion. Big Bend National Park also has a problem with haze. Retired rangers returning to Big Bend are often shocked by how mountain views have deteriorated. Big Bend haze is believed to originate mostly from the industrialized areas of the Texas Gulf Coast and northern Mexico.

El Paso

Of all Texas cities, El Paso suffers for the greatest variety of air pollution problems. In recent years, it has "achieved" nonattainment status for fine particulate matter, carbon monoxide, and ozone; and parts of the El Paso area have had problems with lead. Most of El Paso's problems relate to geography. The city, like Los Angeles and Mexico City, is hemmed in by mountains that restrict atmospheric circulation and permit pollutants to accumulate. El Paso also shares its valley with an even larger city, Ciudad Juárez, and a major army base, Fort Bliss (fig. 10.8). Unpaved Juárez streets, tank activities at Fort Bliss, area

Fɪɢ. 10.8. El Paso and Ciudad Juárez nestled between mountain ranges in Texas and Mexico. Courtesy *Texas Highways.*

refineries, concrete plants, brick factories, and smelters all contribute to the problem.

On the Positive Side

Environmental reports often can be all doom and gloom, but there is some good news.

Eliminating lead from products like paint and gasoline has greatly diminished lead as an environmental problem.

Legislation has been enacted to curb certain practices and encourage recycling. In the past, do-it-yourself oil changers in Texas annually dumped an estimated 20 million gallons of used motor oil on the ground or down drains, but dumping oil is now a violation subject to a hefty fine. Dumping tires and lead-acid batteries is also illegal. These are all recyclable products, as are most of the 19.4 million tons of garbage that Texas citizens and businesses generate each year.

On April 7, 1992, Governor Ann Richards announced an ambitious statewide campaign, designed to get every Texan involved in taking care of the state's environment. Called Clean Texas 2000, it set specific goals for reducing hazardous waste and increasing recycling by the year 2000. Although there is far to go, legislation and fledgling recycling efforts are beginning to make a better future for us all.

There are also encouraging signs from the farm sector. In early 1992, farmers and ranchers from sixty counties lined up voluntarily to turn in more than 197 tons of agricultural pesticides, some inherited from fathers or even grandfathers. Included were 23 tons of arsenic chemicals banned during the 1980s, and 3.9 tons of DDT, banned for use since 1972.

Like other major Texas cities, San Antonio has turned floodprone areas near rivers into green belts, with parks, golf courses, and routes providing access to downtown via elevated highways. The city is working to slake its growing thirst by diverting storm water toward sinkhole openings in the Edwards Aquifer. San Antonio has a long history of transforming abandoned cement quarries from eyesores to assets. No longer sources for cement, old quarries now stand as concrete examples of what can be done with a little imagination and a big hole in the ground. The results include Trinity University, the San Antonio Zoo, the Sunken Gardens, Fiesta Texas, and an eighteen-hole golf course aptly named The Quarry (fig. 10.9).

Along the Gulf Coast, the largest and most productive bay in all of Texas recently was ranked first among Gulf of Mexico estuaries by the U.S. Environmental Protection Agency in terms of total pounds of toxins released per year. Galveston Bay services Houston, the country's third largest shipping port and America's largest oil and petrochemical complex. The Houston Ship Channel once was so polluted that it was devoid of aquatic life (fig. 10.10). A state official showed how volatile the situation had become by striking a match and setting the channel afire. But the Water Quality Act of 1987 created the Galveston Bay National Estuary Program to develop a pollution control plan, and new regulations already have vastly improved the water quality in industrialized portions of the bay. Aquatic life has returned to the ship channel; however, it remains unfit for human consumption.

On the coast, the Galveston sea wall has helped to spawn a thriving tourist industry. Below sea level, marine communities thrive in habitats created around the granite-rock jetties built to protect Galveston's shorelines and passes. Far offshore, platforms built to extract petroleum have created tropical reeflike environments, happily occupied by fish and coated by numerous encrusting organisms. Even in the bays, there are

FIG. 10.9. Fiesta Texas is an imaginative use for an abandoned quarry.
Photo by author.

successes. Although bay dredging has produced huge spoils piles, the islands formed by this activity have created new habitats for colonies of gulls, terns, black skimmers, herons, ibises, and egrets. The only salt-water nesting colony of white pelicans is on a spoils island in the Laguna Madre, and the largest colony of the endangered brown pelican is making a strong comeback in the Corpus Christi ship channel on a spoils bank called, appropriately, Pelican Island. These birds are emerging as victors in the environmental crisis, proving in the process that "to the spoils, go the victors."

Innovative educational curriculums, directed at the newest generation of Texans, have been designed to enhance environmental consciousness and develop the environmental ethic needed to carry Texas safely into the next millennium. If the current generation of adults becomes the last to borrow Earth from their children, then those children will be the first generation in a very long while truly to inherit Earth.

FIG. 10.10. The Houston Ship Channel is a major problem area that has shown recent improvement. Courtesy *Texas Highways.*

References

Autin, W. J. 1984. *Observations and significance of sinkhole development at Jefferson Island.* Geological Pamphlet No. 7. Baton Rouge: Louisiana Geological Survey, Department of Natural Resources. 75p.

Baker, V. 1975. *Flood hazards along the Balcones Escarpment in Central Texas.* Geological Circular 75–5. Austin: Bureau of Economic Geology, University of Texas at Austin. 22p.

Baumgardner, R. W., Jr.; A. D. Hoadley; and A. G. Goldstein. 1982. *Formation of the Wink Sink, a salt dissolution and collapse feature, Winkler County, Texas.* Report of Investigations no. 114. Austin: Bureau of Economic Geology, University of Texas at Austin. 38p.

Brown, L. F., Jr.; R. A. Morton; J. H. McGowen; C. W. Kreitler; and W. L. Fisher. 1974. *Natural hazards of the Texas coastal zone.* Austin: Bureau of Economic Geology, University of Texas at Austin. 19p.

Mullican, W. F., III. 1988. *Subsidence and collapse at Texas salt domes.* Geological Circular 88-2. Austin: Bureau of Economic Geology, University of Texas at Austin. 36p.

Paine, J. G., and R. A. Morton. 1989. *Shoreline and vegetation-line movement, Texas Gulf Coast, 1974 to 1982.* Geological Circular 89-1. Austin: Bureau of Economic Geology, University of Texas at Austin. 50p.

Schroder, E. E.; B. C. Massey; and E. H. Chin. 1987. Floods in Central Texas, August 1–4, 1978. United States Geological Survey Professional Paper 1332. Washington, D.C. 39p.

Simpkins, W. W.; T. C. Gustavson; A. B. Alhades; and A. D. Hoadley. 1981. *Impact of evaporite dissolution and collapse on highways and other cultural features in the Texas Panhandle and Eastern New Mexico.* Geological Circular 81-4. Austin: Bureau of Economic Geology, University of Texas at Austin. 23p.

Texas Water Commission. 1989. *Ground-water quality of Texas: an overview of natural and man-affected conditions.* Texas Water Commission Report 89-01. Austin: Texas Water Commission. 197p., 3 maps.

Appendixes

Appendix A
Texas Gem, Mineral, and Fossil Clubs

Arlington Gem and Mineral Club
4210 Barnett Street
Arlington TX 76017

Austin Gem and Mineral Society
6719 Burnet Lane
Austin TX 78757

Bandera Rockhound Club
Route 1, Box 179
Bandera TX 78003

Big Spring Prospectors Club, Inc.
P.O. Box 1182
Big Spring TX 79721

Brazos Gem and Mineral Society
of Granbury
16420 Edgemere
Pflugerville TX 78660

Central Texas Paleontological Society
16420 Edgemere
Pflugerville TX 78660

Clear Lake Gem and Mineral Society
P.O. Box 58072
Houston TX 77258

Cross Timbers Gem and Mineral Club
271 Hawk St.
Dublin TX 76446

Dallas Gem and Mineral Society, Inc.
P.O. Box 742033
Dallas TX 75374

DeRidder Gem and Mineral Society
Route 3, Box 53-D
Kirbyville TX 75956

East Texas Gem and Mineral Society
416 Hudson
Tyler TX 75701-5511

Faceters' Guild
312 Thornridge
Midland TX 79703

Fort Worth Gem and Mineral Club
P.O. Box 11204
Fort Worth TX 76110-0204

Galveston County Gem and Mineral
Society
3121 Danforth
Texas City TX 77590

Geology Club of San Antonio
218 Sunnycrest
San Antonio TX 78228

Golden Spread Gem and Mineral
Society
P.O. Box 19144
Amarillo TX 79114

Gulf Coast Gem and Mineral Society
P.O. Box 6494
Corpus Christi TX 78411-6494

Highland Lakes Gem and Mineral
Society
25 Fairway Lane
Marble Falls TX 78654

Hi-Plains Gem and Mineral Society
Wayland Baptist University
275 Seventh St.
Plainview TX 79072

Houston Gem and Mineral Society
10805 Brooklet
Houston TX 77099

Lubbock Gem and Mineral Society
Box 6371
Lubbock TX 79493

Magic Valley Gem and Mineral
Society, Inc.
P.O. Box 3004
Edinburg TX 78540

Oak Cliff Gem and Mineral Society
1619 Savoy
Dallas TX 75224

Pine County Gem and Mineral
Society
P.O. Box 203
Pineland TX 75968

Pleasant Oaks Gem and Mineral
Club of Dallas
1401 McDonald Dr.
Garland TX 75041

Rollin' Rock Club, Inc.
Star Route, Box 96
Henrietta TX 76365

Southwest Gem and Mineral Society
P.O. Box 830792
San Antonio TX 78283-0792

Texarkana Gem and Mineral Club
P.O. Box 1196
Texarkana AR 75504

Texas Big Bend Gem and Mineral
Society
205 E. Sul Ross Ave.
Alpine TX 79830

Texas Faceters' Guild
6503 Almeda
Houston TX 77021

Texoma Rockhounds
P.O. Box 2
Blue Ridge TX 75424

Tri-City Gem and Mineral Society
P.O. Box 735
Temple TX 76503

Val Verde Gem and Mineral Society
P.O. Box 1304
Brackettville TX 78832

Victoria Gem and Mineral Society
Park Plaza #7
Port Lavaca TX 77979

Waco Gem and Mineral Club
P.O. Box 8811
Waco TX 76714-8811

Williamson County Gem and Mineral
Society
P.O. Box 422
Georgetown TX 78626

Appendix B
Professional Earth Science Organizations in Texas

An extraordinarily large number of professional earth science organizations exist in Texas. These range from national and international societies to local groups that gather to "talk shop" and promote their science. Local geological societies are of interest for two reasons. First, their guidebooks and other publications commonly are the best sources of geologic information available for specific parts of Texas. These may be technical publications, but most field guidebooks are understandable to folks with just a little earth science background.Second, local societies tend to be dominated by petroleum geologists who know the local geologic setting well, but who also may have worked in far-flung parts of the world. They may be only too happy to tell an organization or class about geologic expeditions to the Middle East, South America, or Borneo, complete with exciting adventures. Some local geologic organizations have educational committees seeking ways to distribute geologic information and member geologists who are willing to lead local field trips.

Amarillo

Amarillo Geophysical Society
P.O. Box 1431
Amarillo TX 79105

Mid-Continent Section
American Association of Petroleum
Geologists*
Box 9839
Amarillo TX 79105

Panhandle Geological Society
P.O. Box 2473
Amarillo TX 79105

Austin

Austin Geological Society
Box 1302
Austin TX 78767

Gulf Coast Association of Geological
Societies*
Box 672
Austin TX 78767

Institute for Geophysics
University of Texas at Austin
8701 N. MoPac Expressway
Austin TX 79759

Texas Bureau of Economic Geology
Box X
University Station
Austin TX 78713

College Station

Ocean Drilling Program*
Texas A&M University Research Park
1000 Discovery Drive
College Station TX 77845

Texas Water Resources Institute
Texas A&M University
College Station TX 77843

Commerce

Geological Society
Department of Earth Sciences
East Texas State University
Commerce TX 75428

Corpus Christi

Coastal Bend Geophysical Society
P.O. Box 2741
Corpus Christi TX 78403

Dallas

Dallas Geological Society
Suite 170
One Energy Square
Dallas TX 75206

Dallas Paleontological Society
Box 710265
Dallas TX 75371

Society of Independent Professional
Earth Scientists*
c/o Diane Finstrom
Suite 170
4925 Greenville Avenue
Dallas TX 75206

El Paso

El Paso Geological Society
Department of Geological Sciences
University of Texas at El Paso
El Paso TX 79968

Graham

Graham Geological Society
P.O. Box 862
Graham TX 76450

Houston

Friends of Mineralogy
14403 Carolcrest
Houston TX 77079

Geophysical Society of Houston
Box 2189
Houston TX 77252

Houston Geological Society
7171 Harwin Drive
Suite 314
Houston TX 77036

Lunar and Planetary Institute*
3303 NASA Road
Houston TX 77058

Lubbock

International Center for Arid and
Semiarid Land Studies*
Mail Stop 1036, Box 41036
Texas Tech University
Lubbock TX 79409

Midland

West Texas Geological Society
P.O. Box 1595
Midland TX 7970

San Angelo

San Angelo Geological Society
P.O. Box 2568
San Angelo TX 76902

San Antonio

South Texas Geological Society
Suite D-100
900 N.E. Loop 410
San Antonio TX 78209

Waco

Baylor Geological Society
Box 97354
Baylor University
Waco TX 76798

South-Central Section
Geological Society of America*
Department of Geology
Baylor University
Waco TX 76798

Wichita Falls

North Texas Geological Society
P.O. Box 1671
Wichita Falls TX 76307

*Regional, national, or international organization with headquarters in Texas
Source: Directory of geoscience organizations. 1994. *Geotimes* 39, no. 10: 14–36.

Appendix C
Careers in Earth Science

Astronomy

If you gaze up in wonder at the night sky and are good at math and science, you may be a candidate to join the small, well-educated group of scientists known as astronomers. There are some 3,500 professional astronomers in the United States—about one-third of world's total. Nearly all have a doctoral degree. About 60 percent work for colleges and universities, where the Ph.D. is generally a basic requirement. University astronomers commonly divide their time between teaching and research. About 30 percent of all astronomers work for the federal government as research scientists at various national observatories or agencies such as the National Aeronautics and Space Administration (NASA). The remaining 10 percent work for private industry or in planetariums and science museums. These jobs may not require the doctoral degree, but they commonly require good writing and public speaking skills.

Astronomers generally work with the light (electromagnetic radiation) reaching Earth from celestial objects. They spend far more time analyzing data than actually working with a telescope. They are generally excellent mathematicians and physicists and are good with computers and instruments. Students should be prepared to take calculus in their first year of college and should obtain a bachelor's degree in astronomy, physics, or math before going to a graduate astronomy program. Astronomy graduate programs exist at Rice University and at the University of Texas at Austin.

Geology

Geologists are curious about Earth. They usually enjoy the outdoors, like to travel, and have a concern for the environment. Geologists reconstruct Earth's geologic history; they study its structure and composition, as well as the physical processes that operate within it and shape its surface. They benefit society by providing information on environmental hazards such as earthquakes, volcanoes, and flooding; and by locating natural resources such as fossil fuels, minerals, and water.

There are approximately 85,000 geoscientists working in the United States. Geologists work for industry, as independent consultants, for federal and state governments, and at universities, colleges, and museums. Nearly half are employed by the petroleum industry, and about one-fourth work either for mining industries or in water resources. Career opportunities currently are increasing in the areas of environmental science and hydrogeology.

Most geologists divide their time between gathering data and specimens in the field, laboratory research on geologic materials, and the compilation of maps and reports in the office. A bachelor's degree in geology is a minimum requirement. A master's degree generally is required for entry-level research positions and for upper-level positions in industry. Nearly all geologists working in advanced research positions and as university professors hold doctoral degrees. Texas has a large number of universities offering undergraduate and graduate degrees in geology.

Meteorology

Most of us think of meteorologists as local television personalities who deliver local weather forecasts. Most meteorologists, however, work behind the scenes. They not only examine current and developing atmospheric conditions to develop forecasts, but also they are engaged in atmospheric research, education, consulting, and administration. Meteorology can be highly interdisciplinary, with meteorologists skilled in such related fields as engineering, agriculture, geological processes, oceanography, biology, or even astronomy and psychology. Industry may employ meteorologists directly or as consultants to assist in developing products or planning operations which might be impacted by climatic conditions. Meteorologists also are employed by the National Oceanic and Atmospheric Administration, the military, universities, and broadcasting corporations.

Today's meteorologists work with sophisticated tools like radar, sophisticated computers, and satellites. Interested high school students should take all the mathematics, physics, chemistry, earth science, and computer science available to them. Not all universities offer degrees in meteorology, and college students may follow one of two paths. They may pursue an undergraduate degree in meteorology, or they may major in a related field such as mathematics or physics, taking what meteorology is available. The latter option is particularly desirable if a graduate degree and a research career is anticipated. The master's degree probably should be considered a minimum requirement for a research position and for maximizing opportunities in other areas of meteorology. Texas has meteorology programs at Texas A&M and Texas Tech universities.

Oceanography

Oceanographers study and describe the world's oceans. They feel an attraction to the sea and the mysteries it still holds. Oceanographers may specialize in physical oceanography (water masses and their movement), chemical oceanography (composition of sea water and the interactions between it and the atmosphere), and biological oceanography (marine life and its complex interrelationships). Geological oceanographers seek to understand the origins of the ocean basins and the patterns and histories of sediment contained in ocean basins.

Although specialized, oceanographers commonly work in interdisciplinary research groups and are knowledgeable in the specialties of their colleagues. Ocean studies are carried out from research ships, submersibles, fixed platforms, underwater laboratories, aircraft, and orbiting satellites.

Oceanographers work for the federal government, private industry, and universities. Virtually all oceanographers have at least a master's degree, and many opportunities are open primarily to those holding a Ph.D. degree. Most oceanographers begin their college education by obtaining a degree in some field of science, mathematics, or engineering. They then concentrate on a specialized field of oceanography at the graduate school level. Two of the top ten or so oceanography programs in the country are located in Texas, at the University of Texas at Austin and Texas A&M University (see chapter 9).

Appendix D
Texas Earth Science Educational Institutions

The forty-three Texas colleges and universities listed below have geoscience departments, and several have programs in astronomy, oceanography, or meteorology as well. Those in italics also offer programs or degrees in the teaching of earth science.

These departments are in the "business" of generating and disseminating information. Formal instruction may be their forte, but many professors are willing to speak to local schools and civic groups, particularly if your thanks include a glowing letter to the college dean. Contact these departments for expert earth science information or for details concerning their degree programs.

Amarillo Junior College. Amarillo; tel. (806) 376-5111.
Angelo State University. San Angelo; tel. (915) 942-2242.
Baylor University. Waco; tel. (817) 755-2361.
Brookhaven College. Farmers Branch; tel. (214) 620-4758.
Corpus Christi State University. Corpus Christi; tel. (512) 994-2681.
Del Mar College. Corpus Christi; tel. (512) 886-1240.
East Texas State University. Commerce; tel. (214) 886-5445.
Hardin-Simmons University. Abilene; tel. (915) 670-1403.
University of Houston. Houston; tel. (713) 743-3399.
Houston Community College System. Houston; tel. (713) 868-0766.
University of Houston Downtown. Houston; tel. (713) 221-8015.
Kilgore College. Kilgore; tel. (214) 984-8531, ext. 253.
Lamar University. Beaumont; tel. (409) 880-8007.
Laredo Junior College. Laredo; tel. (210) 721-5195.
Lee College. Baytown; tel. (713) 427-5611.
McMurry College. Abilene; tel. (915) 691-6599.
Midwestern State University. Wichita Falls; tel. (817) 689-4250.
North Harris County College. Houston; tel. (713) 443-5796.
University of North Texas. Denton; tel. (817) 565-2091.
Odessa College. Odessa; tel. (915) 335-6558.
Rice University. Houston; tel. (713) 527-4880.
Sam Houston State University. Huntsville; tel. (409) 294-1566.
San Antonio College. San Antonio; tel. (512) 733-2828.
South Plains College. Levelland; tel. (806) 894-9611.
Southern Methodist University. Dallas; tel. (214) 768-2750.
Saint Mary's University. San Antonio; tel. (210) 436-3235.
Stephen F. Austin State University. Nacogdoches; tel. (409) 568-3701.
Sul Ross State University. Alpine; tel. (915) 837-8259.
Tarleton State University. Stephenville; tel. (817) 968-9143.
Tarrant County Junior College. Fort Worth; tel. (817) 534-4861, ext. 267.
University of Texas at Arlington. Arlington; tel. (817) 273-2987.
University of Texas at Austin:
    Department of Geological Sciences. Tel. (512) 471-9425.
    Department of Marine Studies. Tel. (512) 749-6777.

Institute for Geophysics. Tel. (512) 471-6156.
University of Texas at Dallas. Richardson; tel. (214) 690-2401.
University of Texas at El Paso. El Paso; tel. (915) 747-5501.
University of Texas—Pan American. Edinburg; tel. (210) 381-3523.
University of Texas, Permian Basin. Odessa; tel. (915) 367-2159.
University of Texas at San Antonio. San Antonio; tel. (210) 691-4455.
Texas A&M University, Kingsville. Kingsville; tel. (512) 595-3310.
Texas A&M University. College Station:
   Center for Tectonophysics. Tel. (409) 845-3251.
   Department of Geology. Tel. (409) 845-2451.
   Department of Geophysics. Tel. (409) 845-6780.
   Department of Meteorology. Tel. (409) 845-7671.
   Department of Oceanography. Tel. (409) 845-7211.
Texas Christian University. Fort Worth; tel. (817) 921-7270.
Texas Tech University. Lubbock; tel. (806) 742-3102.
Trinity University. San Antonio; tel. (210) 736-7606.
West Texas State University. Canyon; tel. (806) 656-2570.

Appendix E
Educational Resource Material

Earth science organizations listed by subject area below all provide free or inexpensive resource material to educational institutions. Call them or write (on school stationery) for information on specific offerings.

Astronomy and Space

American Astronomical Society, c/o Charles R. Tolbert, Education Office, Box 3818, University Station, Charlottesville VA 22903-0818; (804) 924-7955

Astronomical Society of the Pacific, Catalog Request Department, 390 Ashton Avenue, San Francisco CA 94112; (415) 337-1100

Harvard-Smithsonian Center for Astrophysics, 60 Garden St., Cambridge MA 02138; (617) 495-7461

Lunar and Planetary Institute, Order Department, 3303 NASA Road #1, Houston TX 77058; (713) 486-2172

NASA Johnson Space Center, Education Officer, Houston TX 77058

NASA Johnson Space Center, Teacher Resource Center, AP42, Houston TX 77058; (713) 483-8696

NASA Spacelink: The computer access number is (205) 895-0028. First-time users must log in as NEWUSER (Password NEWUSER)

Sky and Telescope Magazine, Sky Publishing Corporation, 49 Bay State Rd., Cambridge MA 02138

Star Date, University of Texas at Austin, RLM 15.308, Austin TX 78712;
(512) 471-5285

Geology

American Gas Association, Educational Programs, 1515 Wilson Boulevard,
Arlington VA 22209; (703) 841-

Center for Earth Science Education, 4220 King Street, Alexandria VA 22302;
(800) 336-4764

American Geophysical Union, Customer Service, 2000 Florida Avenue NW,
Washington DC 20009; (202) 462-6903

Federal Emergency Management Agency, Earthquake Program, 500 C Street
SW, Washington DC 20472; Attention: Marilyn MacCabe

National Earth Science Teachers Association, 14 Science Department, Lansing
Community College, 419 Washington Street, Lansing MI 48901

U.S. Department of Energy, National Energy Information Center, EL-231, Room
1F-048, Forrestal Building, 1000 Independence Avenue SW, Washington DC 20585; (202) 586-8800

U.S. Department of Energy, Office of Communications, Office of Fossil Energy,
1000 Independence Avenue SW, Washington DC 20585

U.S. Geological Survey, Geological Inquiries Group, 907 National Center,
Reston VA 22092; (703) 648-4383

Oceanography

National Association of Biology Teachers, 11250 Roger Bacon Drive #19, Reston
VA 22090; (703) 471-1134

The Oceanography Society, 1701 K Street NW, Suite 300, Washington DC
20006-1509

Water and the Environment

American Ground Water Trust, 6375 Riverside Drive, Dublin OH 43017;
(614) 761-2215

American Institute of Professional Geologists, 7828 Vance Drive, Suite 103,
Arvada CO 80003; (303) 431-0831

Climate Protection Institute, 5833 Balmoral Drive, Oakland CA 94619;
(415) 531-0100

Texas Natural Resources Conservation Commission, Office of Public Information, P.O. Box 13087, Austin TX 78711; 1-800-458-9796

U.S. Environmental Protection Agency, Public Information Center, 401 M
Street SW, Washington D.C. 20460

U.S. Geological Survey, Hydrologic Information Unit, Water Resources Division,
419 National Center, Reston VA 22092; (703) 648-6818

ZPG (Zero Population Growth), 1400 16th Street NW, Suite 320, Washington
DC 20036

Weather and Climate

American Meteorological Society, 45 Beacon Street, Boston MA 02108;
(617) 227-2425

Educational Weather Services, 1522 Baylor Avenue, Rockville MD 20850;
(301) 762-7669

For Spacious Skies, 54 Webb Street, Lexington MA 02173; (617) 862-4289

U.S. National Oceanic and Atmospheric Administration, National Climatic
Center, Federal Building, Asheville NC 28801; (704) 259-0682

Appendix F
Texas Points of Earth Science Interest

The points of earth science interest listed below generally are arranged according to the Texas physiographic province in which they occur and in a sequence
progressing westward. Please note that there has been no attempt to list hours
of operation. It is always advisable to call ahead.

Texas Gulf Coastal Plain

Beaumont
Spindletop/Gladys City Boomtown. Next to Lamar University, off U.S. Highway
69 South at University Drive. The 1901 birthplace of the modern petroleum industry and a re-creation of the world's first oil boom town.
Texas Energy Museum. Downtown, at 600 Main Street. Industry and Lamar
University collections documenting Spindletop and the development of
the petroleum industry.

Bryan
Brazos Valley Museum of Natural Science. Brazos Center, 3232 Briarcrest
Drive. Natural history of the Brazos Valley, including fossil mammoths
and a slide show on the extinction of the dinosaurs.
Tektites. Strange glassy objects believed to be the chilled produce of molten
rock expelled from large meteorite impacts. Found south of the Bryan
area, from Dime Box to Bedias.

Clarksville
Clarksville received 109.38 inches of rain in 1873, a Texas record.

Clute
Brazosport Museum of Natural Science. 400 College Drive. Includes fossils, rocks,
minerals, an aquarium, and the largest shell collection in the
Southwest.

Corpus Christi
Corpus Christi Museum of Science and History. Bayfront Arts and Science Park, 1900 N. Chaparral. Gulf of Mexico natural history, shells, dinosaur exhibits, and artifacts.
Padre Island National Seashore. Across the John F. Kennedy Causeway from Corpus Christi. 113-mile-long barrier island, including an 80-mile undeveloped zone.
Texas State Aquarium. 2710 N. Shoreline Boulevard, Surfside Exit from U.S. Highway 181. Gulf of Mexico habitats, ranging from estuaries to offshore. More than 250 species of sea life, in over 350,000 gallons of sea water.

Damon
Damon Mound, rising 83 feet above the flat coastal plain, is the surface expression of an enormous, subsurface pillar of salt. Like Spindletop, Damon Mound has produced millions of barrels of petroleum.

Galveston
Galveston Island. Contains 32 miles of sandy beach and the *Galveston Seawall,* built in 1902 following the disastrous hurricane of 1900. Large stone blocks (rip rap) along the beach and in jetties protect the beach from erosion. The blocks are composed of Precambrian granite quarried near Marble Falls. The island also contains *Galveston Island State Park,* which extends from the Gulf shore to salt marshes of the Bay. Galveston is home port for the JOIDES *Resolution* (see chapter 9), one of the world's most advanced ocean research vessels. Look for the derrick on the deck of a ship named *SEDCO.*
Moody Gardens. Near Galveston Island State Park. Includes a tour showing a variety of animals (Seaside Safari) and a mineral display.

Gladewater
The Mexia-Gladewater area is seismically active. The 1957 Gladewater quake had an estimated Richter magnitude of 4.7.

Goliad
A tornado on May 18, 1902, destroyed the town of Goliad, killing 114 persons, a record for Texas tornadoes (shared with Waco).

Grand Saline
Salt Palace. U.S. Highway 80 at Main Street. Constructed in 1975, this salt-block building contains salt-related items and salt mine memorabilia. A massive dome underlying the city constitutes one of the nation's largest salt sources.

Houston
Houston Museum of Natural Science. 1 Hermann Circle (a short distance north of the Astrodome). Includes the Burke Baker Planetarium; the Wiess Hall of Petroleum Science and Technology; and the Lillie and Roy Cullen Gallery of Earth Science, with fantastic displays of rare gems, minerals, and fossils, including various dinosaurs and a 70-foot-long *Diplodocus.*
Lyndon B. Johnson Space Center. In far Southwest Houston, 3 miles east of Interstate Highway 45 on NASA Road 1. Includes Mission Control Center for our nation's manned space program, a visitor center, Rocket

Park with a giant Saturn V rocket, astronaut training facilities, and the Lunar Sample Laboratory containing the world's largest collection of moon rocks and meteorites.

Space Center Houston. Adjacent to the Johnson Space Center. Disney-designed. Space capsules and other artifacts, training simulators, hands-on activities, and an IMAX theater. There is a charge for admission. Tel. 1-800-972-0369.

Humble

Humble Historical Museum. 219 Main Street. Includes oil-field equipment used after the discovery of petroleum here in 1904. Founding location for the Humble Oil and Refining Company, which later became Exxon.

Indianola

Indianola was largely destroyed by a hurricane in 1875 and then was erased from the map forever by a hurricane in 1886.

Kendleton

On May 2, 1939, a fireball meteor exploded over Kendleton. After several minutes, fragments—some weighing several pounds—fell across the area.

Kilgore

East Texas Oil Museum. Kilgore College campus, U.S. Highway 259 at Ross Street. Kilgore is at the center of the huge East Texas Oil Field, discovered in 1930. The museum's dioramas and films recreate daily life during Kilgore's boom days. Geological exhibits include a simulated 3,800-foot descent to oil-rich formations below.

World's Richest Acre. Texas Highway 135, Business Route, at Main and Commerce Streets. About 1.2 acres. The twenty-four wells drilled here produced more than 2.5 million barrels of oil. Kilgore once had more than 1,200 oil wells within its city limits. Kilgore, alone, could have supplied the nation's petroleum needs for the decade of the 1940s.

Kingsville

John E. Conner Museum. Texas A&M University at Kingsville campus. Historical museum with some fossil mammals, including mammoth bones.

Moscow

Dinosaur Gardens. U.S. Highway 59 near intersection of F.M. Road 62. On 1,000-foot forest path, see life-sized replicas, complete with sounds, of the unlikely combination of dinosaurs and saber-toothed tigers.

Nacogdoches

L. T. Barret Memorial. Campus of Stephen F. Austin State University. Memorial to the man who, in 1866, drilled the first Texas oil well.

Palestine

Scientific Balloon Base. NASA-operated base periodically launches balloons to study the upper atmosphere. Tours arranged. Tel. (903) 729-0271.

Pleasanton
Earthquakes measuring 3.9 and 4.2 on the Richter scale shook the Pleasanton-Jourdanton area on March 3, 1984, and on April 9, 1993.

Port Aransas
Mustang Island State Park. 14 miles south of Port Aransas via Texas Highway 361, accessible from Corpus Christi or by toll-free ferry from Aransas Pass. 3,703 acres of barrier island at the southern end of Mustang Island.
University of Texas Marine Science Institute. Along the ship channel between Mustang and San Jose islands. Laboratory and research facility with oceanographic displays and publications. Educational tours can be arranged by mail: P.O. Box 1267, Port Aransas TX 78373-1267.

Port O'Connor
Matagorda Island State Park and Wildlife Management Area. 7 miles south of the city, across Espirito Santo and San Antonio bays. A barrier island accessible only by private or chartered boat.

Richmond
Brazos Bend State Park. 20 miles south via F.M. Road 762. Includes George Observatory and a 36-inch telescope open to the public on Saturday evenings.

South Padre Island
Twenty-five miles northeast of Brownsville, with causeway access from Port Isabel.

Tyler
Hudnall Planetarium. At Tyler Junior College, east of downtown just off Texas Highway 64. Planetarium and replicas of space vehicles.

Victoria
Texas Zoo. 110 Memorial Drive. This collection of Texas animals also has mammoth and mastodon bones on display.

Edwards Plateau and the Central Mineral Region (Including Cities Adjacent to the Balcones Escarpment)

Austin
Austin Nature Center. Nature Center Drive, in Southwest Austin. Exhibits in science, natural history, and botany.
Bureau of Economic Geology. Balcones Research Center, Building 130, 10100 Burnet Road, in Northwest Austin. A wealth of geologic literature at reasonable rates, and a public service geologist to answer questions. Displays include rocks, minerals, meteorites, and tektites.
Congress Avenue Bridge. Summer site of the nation's largest urban bat colony. Information at the Four Seasons Hotel.
Lyndon B. Johnson Library and Museum. 2313 Red River Street. Exhibits include a moon rock.
Pilot Knob. Southeast of Austin on U.S. Highway 183, near Bergstrom Air Force Base. Pilot Knob is a deeply eroded, extinct Cretaceous volcano. The

surrounding farm land is underlain by ash from the volcano, and an adjacent limestone ridge is a fossil reef fringing this Cretaceous-age volcanic island. The reef-rock and underlying ash also can be seen at McKinney Falls State Park just north of Pilot Knob.

State Capitol Building. Contains white blocks of limestone quarried locally but was mostly built from 15,000 train car loads of pink granite quarried from Granite Mountain near Marble Falls.

Texas Memorial Museum. University of Texas campus area, 2400 Trinity Street. Exhibits include excellent examples of rocks, minerals, and meteorites, including fragments from the Odessa iron meteorite. Fossils include *Quezalcoatlus,* the Onion Creek Mosasaur, mastodons, a giant ground sloth, various dinosaur bones, and an armadillo as big as a chest freezer.

Texas Museum of Natural History. 600 Congress Avenue, 2nd floor pavilion. Exhibits devoted to paleontology, rocks, and minerals.

Zilker Park. Southwest Austin. Includes Barton Springs and a 1,000-foot-long spring-fed pool, into which water gushes from along a fault cutting the Edwards Aquifer. Dinosaur tracks are located in the park's botanical gardens.

Bend

Gorman Cave. Colorado Bend State Park, west of Lampasas via Rural Route 580 and Rural Route 581. Guided tours of the cave are available; reservations are recommended.

Blanco

Dinosaur tracks and trails of a giant Sauropod are found in the bed of the Blanco River, about 3 miles west of town on F.M. Road 1623 and especially where Blanco County Road 103 crosses the river. Land around is private.

Boerne Area

Cascade Caverns. 5 miles southeast of Boerne off U.S. Highway 87, or 14 miles northwest of San Antonio on Interstate Highway 10 (exit 543). Open since 1932, this cave features a 100-foot subterranean waterfall.

Cave Without a Name. 11 miles northeast of Boerne, 6 miles via F.M. Road 474 then right 4.6 miles on Kreutzberg Road. A contest to name the cave was won by a boy who said, "This cave is too pretty to name." Cave has stalactites, stalagmites, and soda straws.

Brackettville

Kickapoo Cavern State Park. 23 miles north on F.M. Road 674. 2000-foot-long Green Cave is home to about one million Mexican free-tail bats. Tours may be arranged; call (210) 563-2342 for information.

Del Rio

San Felipe Springs and Moore Park. Spring issues some 90 million gallons of water daily.

Enchanted Rock State Park

Eighteen miles north of Fredericksburg off F.M. Road 965. Enchanted Rocka National Natural Landmark, is the country's second largest granite exfoliation dome (after Stone Mountain, Georgia). The 500-foot-high dome exhibits many features characteristic of exposed granitic igneous rocks.

Eola

Barrow Museum. 4.5 miles east on F.M. Road 765. Early farm and ranch collection includes a gem and mineral collection.

Georgetown

Inner Space Caverns. Off Interstate Highway 35, 1 mile south of Georgetown or 27 miles north of Austin. Formed by dissolution along fractures associated with the Balcones Fault system, the cave was discovered during construction of I-35. The owners use lighting and acoustics to dramatize the cave's natural beauty. The cave also features an entrance via inclined rail "subway" and Ice Age mammal remains.

Hondo

Dinosaur Tracks. 23.5 miles north of Highway 90 on F.M. Road 462. Exhibit of fossil dinosaur tracks in the bed of Hondo Creek.

Knippa

Traprock quarry. On U.S. Highway 90, 12 miles east of Uvalde. The basaltic rock shows well-developed columnar jointing, a feature formed during slow cooling and contraction of the lava.

Longhorn Cavern State Park

Longhorn Cavern. About 12 miles southeast of Buchanan Dam, or 11 miles southwest of Burnet on Park Road 4, 6 miles off U.S. Highway 281. Officially opened in 1932, the cave has yielded bones, including those of a grizzly bear, bobcat, elephant, and bison. Two human skeletons, believed to be the remains of an Indian and a Confederate soldier, also have been found.

Marlin

Local wells produce geothermal water at 147 degrees Fahrenheit, to heat a local hospital.

Mason

Mason Country is known to mineral collectors throughout the nation for gem-quality blue topaz, the official Texas state gem.

New Braunfels

Comal Springs. A major discharge point for the Edwards Aquifer and source for the Comal River. The Comal River flows only 2.5 miles before entering the Guadalupe River. The Comal is the shortest river in Texas, and no other U.S. river of this length or shorter carries as much water.

Natural Bridge Caverns. Between San Antonio and New Braunfels, off Interstate Highway 35 via F.M. Road 3009. This cave, now a U.S. National Landmark, was discovered in 1960 and named for a 60-foot natural limestone bridge at the entrance. The cave is nicely decorated and features large rooms and an underground stream.

Ozona

Crockett County Museum. Highway 290 and Avenue E. In the basement of the county courthouse. Small historical museum includes some area invertebrate fossils and a few mammoth bones.

Pedernales Falls State Park

Nine miles east of Johnson City on F.M. Road 3232. The falls formed over tilted Paleozoic limestone strata.

San Angelo

Angelo State University Planetarium. On campus, in the Nursing-Physical Science Building. Nation's fourth largest university planetarium.

Concho River Pearls. Concho River and local shops. Pearls form in freshwater clams and range in color from pink to rich purple. Pearl hunters must obtain a permit from the Texas Parks and Wildlife Department.

San Antonio

San Pedro Spring. Located in San Pedro Park, the oldest public park in Texas (established 1734). Natural spring issues from along a fault in the Austin chalk.

Sea World of Texas. West of San Antonio, at Ray Ellison Drive and Westover Hills Boulevard. This large theme park features marine mammals and includes an immense salt-water aquarium which can be viewed through glass walls.

Water Museum. San Antonio Water Board, 1000 Commerce Street. Exhibits include mementos of San Antonio's early water system, including displays of *acequias* (irrigation canals) from Spanish colonial days and contemporary diagrams of the Edwards Aquifer.

Witte Memorial Museum. 3801 Broadway. Exhibits relating to the natural history of Texas, including some fossils and dinosaur exhibits.

San Marcos

Aquarena Springs. Aquarena Springs Drive Exit from Interstate Highway 35. Source for the spring-fed San Marcos River and a major discharge point for the Edwards Aquifer. Of interest are several endangered species, an underwater archeological site, and a swimming pig named Ralph.

Wonder World Caverns. Bishop Street. Discovered in 1893 and billed as "earthquake-formed," the cave formed along the Balcones Fault system.

San Saba

The area is noted for its native building stone and mineral collecting. Details at the Chamber of Commerce in the county courthouse.

Sattler (Near Canyon Lake, north of San Antonio)

Dinosaur Flats. 2 miles southwest of town on F.M. Road 2673. Site of hundreds of dinosaur tracks exposed in Cretaceous limestone and uncovered by excavators in 1982. A religious group offers an alternative interpretation.

Sequin

Fiedler Memorial Museum. Langner Hall, on the campus of Texas Lutheran College. Includes area rocks, minerals, and fossils.

Sonora

Caverns of Sonora. About 8 miles southwest of Sonora off Interstate Highway 10 (exit 392) on F.M. Road 1989. Considered to be one of the most beautifully decorated caves in the world. Amazing profusion of delicate crystal growths and spectacular dripstone formations, including rare helictites and soda straws.

Thrall

Thrall is the unofficial site of the heaviest rainfall ever recorded in United States history, 36.40 inches in just eighteen hours.

Uvalde

Bee Bluff Impact Site. 12 miles south of Uvalde on Highway 83. Probable ancient meteorite impact site. The structure occupies a 1.5 mile circular area just past the Nueces River. Look for undisturbed sandstone beds passing into tilted and broken rock formations.

Asphalt Mines. 8 miles south of U.S. Highway 90 on Rural Route 1022, in the Cline and Blewett area. The largest natural asphalt mines in Texas, perhaps in the United States. Tar occurs in porous, fossiliferous limestone in just the right proportions to be quarried, crushed, and used as pavement.

Waco

A tornado on May 11, 1953, tore through the heart of downtown Waco killing 114 persons, a record for Texas tornadoes (shared with Go-liad).

Strecker Museum. Sid Richardson Hall, Baylor University. Exhibits include geological displays with a giant marine turtle and part of a plesiosaur skeleton.

Grand and Black Prairies

Cleburne

Layland Museum. Carnegie Library, 201 N. Caddo. Displays include fossils.

Clifton

Bosque Memorial Museum. South Avenue Q and West Ninth Street. Displays include a Texas mineral and fossil collection.

Dallas

State Fair Park. Central Dallas. Exhibits on the grounds include an aquarium, the Museum of Natural History with excellent fossil displays, and Science Place I and II (with planetarium).

Denison

Denison Dam at Lake Texoma. 1 mile north on U.S. Highway 75A. A tour of the powerhouse includes an exhibit of fossils unearthed during dam construction.

Fort Worth

Fort Worth Museum of Science and History. 1501 Montgomery Street, Amon Carter Square. Exhibits include geology, paleontology, and astronomy in the Nobel Planetarium.

Glen Rose

Comanche Peak Nuclear Power Plant. A visitor center explains nuclear power.

Dinosaur Valley State Park. 5 miles west of town off U.S. Highway 67 on F.M.
    Road 205. The first and best-preserved Sauropod dinosaur tracks in
    Texas are found in the bed of the Paluxy River. The visitor center has
    full-sized models of a vegetarian Sauropod and a carnivorous Theropod
    dinosaur.

Somervell County Historical Museum. Elm and Vernon Streets. Items include
    fossils.

McKinney

Heard Natural Science Museum and Wildlife Sanctuary. South 2 miles on Texas
    Highway 5, east 1 mile on F.M. Road 1378. Natural history exhibits in-
    clude geology.

Vernon

Red River Valley Museum. 4400 College Drive. Exhibits include history of oil
    industry in Wilbarger County.

The Western Company Museum. 6100 Western Place, 1st floor of the Western
    Company corporate headquarters. Display of astrophotography, fossils,
    and oil field equipment.

North-Central Plains

Archer

Archer City Museum. Old jail on the corner of Sycamore and Pecan. A small
    county museum with Permian fossils, including some early land verte-
    brates.

Burkburnett

Felty Outdoor Oil Museum. On Gresham Road (F.M. Road 240). Oil field equip-
    ment from boom days following the 1912 discovery of oil. This discov-
    ery served as the basis for the 1941 Clark Gable–Spencer Tracy film
    "Boomtown."

Ranger

McClesky No. 1. Granite monument at downtown railroad depot. Marks the
    site of the 1917 gusher that touched off Ranger's boom-town days.

Roaring Ranger Museum. Main and Commerce Streets. Converted depot
    houses oil boom days artifacts and photos.

Seymour

The temperature in Seymour on August 12, 1936, reached 120 degrees Fahren-
    heit, the highest temperature ever recorded in Texas.

Thurber

On Interstate Highway 20, 70 miles west of Fort Worth. Former site of a coal
    mine and high-grade clay for Thurber bricks. Photos are found in the
    local restaurant, and the adjacent service station is a replica of the place
    where freight cars were unloaded by tipping (a mine tipple).

Wichita Falls

On April 10, 1979, Wichita Falls was hit by the most destructive tornado in Texas history. The twister destroyed over 3,000 homes and left 42 people dead; 1,740 injured; and an estimated 20,000 homeless.

Museum and Art Center. 2 Eureka Circle. Contains a planetarium.

Southern High Plains (Includes adjacent oil-producing sites)

Amarillo

Don Harrington Discovery Center. 1200 Steit Drive. Museum and planetarium. Displays include "Aquariums of the World" and a black hole. Also, the Helium Monument, a six-story stainless-steel column, commemorates the discovery of helium, a gas found locally in the world's greatest quantity.

Big Lake

Santa Rita No. 1. Historical marker 4 miles west of town on U.S. Highway 67. Actual 1923 discovery-well site. Oil production from University of Texas lands around Big Lake made the University of Texas at Austin one of the richest schools in the nation. The site includes an oil derrick and some original equipment.

Canyon

Palo Duro Canyon State Park. 12 miles east of Canyon on Texas Highway 217 and Park Road 5. The canyon contains brilliant multicolored strata exposed by erosion of the Prairie Dog Town Fork of the Red River into the Llano Estacado or Texas High Plains.

Panhandle-Plains Historical Museum. Campus of West Texas State University. Old West exhibits include excellent fossil displays and the Don Harrington Petroleum Wing, which covers geology and petroleum production.

Fritch

Alibates Flint Quarries National Monument. 36 miles north of Amarillo and 6 miles south of Fritch, just off Texas Highway 136. Tours guided by Park Service personnel, of flint quarries used by Indians from 12,000 years ago until about 1870.

Iraan

Historical marker in city park gives details of the 1928 gusher that became one of the largest producing oil wells in North America.

Fantasyland. On U.S. Highway 190 adjacent to the city park. Contains giant statues of characters from the comic strip, Alley Oop. The strip was created by V. T. Hamlin while he lived in Iraan, and its success probably increased the widespread misconception that cave man and dinosaur coexisted.

Iraan Archeological Museum. Fantasyland Park. Contains excellent fossil exhibits and oil field relics.

Kermit

Pioneer Park. 4 blocks north of Texas Highway 302 at eastern city limits. Outdoor museum includes an old wooden cable-tool drilling rig.

Lubbock

Lubbock Lake Landmark State Historical Park. Northwest Lubbock, access from
     intersection of U.S. Highway 84 and Loop 289. Important archeological
     site, with artifacts from approximately 11,000 B.C. to recent times ex-
     hibited in the interpretive center. Also exhibited are mammoth, horse,
     camel, giant bison, and giant armadillo fossil remains.
Museum of Texas Tech University. 4th Street and Indiana Avenue. Exhibits
     include a planetarium, the natural history of arid and semiarid lands,
     dinosaur bones, and fabulous jades and ivories that once belonged to
     Helena Rubinstein.

McCamey

Mendoza Trail Museum. On U.S. Highway 67 East. Includes fossils and memen-
     tos of McCamey's boom-town days.

Miami

Roberts County Museum. Restored Santa Fe Railroad Depot on U.S. Highway
     60 in town. Collections include prehistoric archaeological artifacts and
     fossils.

Midland

Museum of the Southwest Complex. 1705 W. Missouri. Complex includes a
     children's museum with a planetarium and astronomy exhibits.
Permian Basin Petroleum Museum, Library, and Hall of Fame. 1500 Interstate
     Highway 20 West. Includes historic items, displays, a slide show, geo-
     logic information on the Permian Basin, and the world's largest collec-
     tion of antique drilling equipment.

Monahans

Million Barrel Museum. On U.S. Highway 80, 1.5 miles east of city. Antique oil
     field equipment and a huge converted oil-storage tank which serves as
     museum.
Monahans Sandhills State Park. Interstate Highway 20/U.S. Highway 80, 5
     miles east of town. 3,840 acres of sand dunes, a museum, and an inter-
     pretive center.

Odessa

Ector County Coliseum. Andrews Highway and 42nd Street. Just north of the
     coliseum is a recreated cable-tool drilling rig with adjacent driller's
     shack, housing photographs and relics of the West Texas oil-boom days.
Odessa Meteor Crater. West of Odessa on Interstate Highway 20, exit at Meteor
     Crater Road and follow the signs. Not spectacular but an authentic me-
     teor crater nonetheless. The mostly filled, 500-foot-wide main crater
     resulted from a cluster of iron meteorites that fell about 20,000 years ago.

Plainview

Llano Estacado Museum. 1900 W. 8th Street, on campus of Wayland Baptist
     University. Exhibits include archeological artifacts, gems and minerals,
     and the "Easter Elephant," a prehistoric mammoth skull and tusk
     found in 1988 near the community of Easter.

Quanah
Copper Breaks State Park. Off Texas Highway 6, 13 miles south of Quanah on the Pease River. Rugged topography (breaks) carved into the High Plains "Cap Rock" exposes brilliantly colored Permian rocks containing some copper.

Quitaque
Caprock Canyons State Park. 50 miles south of Amarillo and 3.5 miles north of Quitaque on F.M. Road 1065. 13,960 acres of the exposed "Cap Rock" edge of the Southern High Plains. Rock strata are the same as at Palo Duro Canyon, and there is an interpretive exhibit explaining the 250 million years of geologic history represent by the rocks. In 1912, Yale University paleontologists unearthed Ice-Age horses, camels, mammoths, giant ground sloths, and bears where Highway 86 passes the head of Rock Creek near here.

Rankin
Rankin Museum. 200 W. Fifth Street. Historic Yates Hotel, built by oil tycoon Ira Yates, includes a geological and shell exhibit.

Seminole
The temperature in Seminole on February 8, 1933, plunged to –23 degrees Fahrenheit, a Texas record (shared with the town of Tulia to the north).

Shamrock
Blarney Stone. Elmore Park. A genuine fragment of the Blarney Stone from the ruins of Blarney Castle, County Cork, Ireland. Irish legend has it that kissing the Blarney Stone gives one the "gift of gab."

Stanton
Martin County Historical Museum. Broadway at Convent Street. Exhibits includes the history of local oil development.

Tulia
The temperature in Tulia on February 12, 1899, plunged to –23 degrees Fahrenheit, a Texas record (shared with the town of Seminole to the south).

Trans-Pecos Texas

Alpine
Museum of the Big Bend. At Sul Ross State University. Displays include information on dinosaurs and agate.
Woodward Agate Ranch. 16 miles south of Alpine on Texas Highway 118. A popular commercial agate and opal hunting site.

Balmorhea
San Solomon Springs. One of the world's largest spring-fed pools is located 4 miles south of U.S. Highway 290, at Balmorhea State Park. A historic watering hole and home of two fish on the endangered species list. The water originates miles to the south in the Davis Mountains and flows at the rate of 22–26 million gallons per day.

Big Bend National Park
801,163 acres of marvelously varied and wonderfully exposed geology. Fossil
beds and mixing zone for species from the Chihuahua desert, Rocky
Mountains, and Mexican highlands. Geologic exhibits at Panther Junction.

Big Bend Ranch State Natural Area
264,000 more acres of Big Bend country, still in the development stage. The
area includes the *Solitario,* a rare exposure of the Ouachita foldbelt
uplifted in a remarkably circular fashion, probably by intrusion of
magma in the form of a laccolith. Over 500 million years of geologic
history exposed.

Davis Mountains
University of Texas McDonald Observatory. At Mt. Locke, 16 miles northwest of
Fort Davis via Texas Highway 118 and Spur 78. One of the world's great
astronomical observatories. The complex contains a visitor center with
numerous programs and exhibits.

El Paso
El Paso Centennial Museum. Campus of University of Texas at El Paso (UTEP),
at University Avenue and Wiggins Road. Displays includes geologic
topics.

Fort Stockton
Annie Riggs Memorial Museum. 301 S. Main. Two rooms in this restored hotel
display geological specimens.
Dinosaur footprints are found in a dry creekbed next to a small picnic area 7
miles north of Interstate Highway 10 on Highway 385.

Guadalupe Mountains National Park
Contains Guadalupe Peak, the state's highest point. An exposed remnant of the
great Capitan Reef, which in late Paleozoic time extended for nearly
400 miles around the margin of the Delaware Basin.

Marathon
Surrounded by mountains, the Marathon Basin is widely known among
geologists for its exposures of folded Paleozoic rocks of the Ouachita
foldbelt.

Marfa
Reported for over 100 years and still defying explanation, the "Marfa lights"
occasionally can be seen from the prime viewing area 9 miles east of
the city on U.S. Highway 90, where a historical marker gives details.

Salt Flat
U.S. Highway 62/180. This town (pop. 35) lies in the shadow of the Guadalupe
Mountains and is near extensive surface salt deposits left by dried playa
lakes.

Sanderson
A flood spilling out of Three-Mile Draw overwhelmed Sanderson on June 11,
1965, causing 26 deaths.

Shafter

Highway 67 between Presidio and Marfa. Shafter is a ghost town but was once an active silver-mining community producing the bulk of Texas' silver and gold.

Study Butte

On Texas Highway 118, at the western edge of Big Bend National Park. The butte is an igneous intrusion which has metamorphosed the surrounding rock. The small town originated at the turn of the century, following the discovery of rich mercury deposits. Rock hounds still find cinnabar and agate.

Terlingua

On Texas Highway 117, just west of Study Butte and Big Bend National Park. Now largely a ghost town, but this site saw the processing of millions of dollars of mercury ore (cinnabar).

Lajitas Museum. On Highway 170, west of Terlingua. General museum with some dinosaur bones and many Cretaceous invertebrate fossils.

Valentine

1931 site of the largest known Texas earthquake. The main shock had an estimated Richter magnitude of 6.0.

Van Horn

On Interstate Highway 10, southeast of El Paso. Surrounding mountains contain rare Texas exposures of Precambrian rocks, as well as abandoned gold, silver, and copper mines.

Index